MEN AGAINST THE SEA

Library and Archives Canada Cataloguing in Publication

Prim, Joseph, 1927-
Men against the sea : ships lost in the Newfoundland foreign trade / Joe Prim and Michael McCarthy.

Includes bibliographical references and index.
ISBN 1-894463-56-0

1. Shipwrecks. 2. Ships--Newfoundland and Labrador.
I. McCarthy, Michael J., 1932- II. Title.

G525.P75 2004 910.4'52 C2004-906087-2

PRINTED IN CANADA

All royalties from this book are donated to the Shriners Hospital for Children, Boston Burn Unit.

FLANKER PRESS LTD.
P.O. BOX 2522, STATION C
ST. JOHN'S, NL CANADA A1C 6K1
TOLL FREE: 1-866-739-4420
TELEPHONE: (709) 739-4477 FAX: (709) 739-4420
WWW.FLANKERPRESS.COM

Canada

We acknowledge the financial support of the Government of Canada through the Book Publishing Industry Development Program (BPIDP) for our publishing program.

We also acknowledge financial assistance from the Government of Newfoundland and Labrador for marketing initiatives.

MEN AGAINST THE SEA

Ships Lost in the Newfoundland Foreign Trade

Captain Joe Prim
and
Michael McCarthy

Flanker Press Ltd.
St. John's, NL
2004

Cover Credit

This book's cover, painted by Matthew Prim, Jr., depicts German Armed Merchant Raider *Moewe* in pursuit of Crosbies-owned tern schooner *Jean* off the coast of Portugal in 1917.

Matthew Prim, Sr. ran away from school in St. John's at the age of thirteen and stowed away on the *Jean*, which was bound to Pernambuco, Brazil, with a cargo of dried fish. When discharged at that port they loaded tobacco for Lisbon. Portugal, from which port they were to load salt for a return trip to Newfoundland. Before that could happen, they were intercepted off the Portuguese coast by the German Raider *Moewe*. Their vessel was sunk, their crew taken prisoners of war and transported by the *Moewe* to Germany and interned for the remainder of the war.

The SS *Moewe* was the most successful German Raider during the First World War. She sank thirty-eight British and Allied vessels, sometimes operating to the eastern edge of the Grand Banks, and twice ran the British blockade in and out of Germany.

The profile of the *Moewe* on this book's cover was taken from 1917 photos.

DEDICATION

This book is dedicated to the memory of the late F. Burnham Gill J.P. who as a Newfoundland Ranger, Newsman and Provincial Archivist served the interests of all Newfoundlanders. As head of the Provincial Archives he did much to direct the reorganization of the archives holdings and made them more readily available to all persons engaged in research about Newfoundland. His personal help to researchers was invaluable and on-going. His contribution to making Newfoundland history and cultural matters available to enthusiasts was acknowledged by the Newfoundland Government in 1982 when they named the new Records Management Centre at Pleasantville, "The Burnham Gill Records Management Centre." On this occasion Premier Brian Peckford praised Mr. Gill for his work in organizing the Newfoundland Provincial Archives saying:

> Mr. Gill, Government is very grateful to you. We appreciate your contribution during your decade of service as Provincial Archivist, and thus we are pleased to name this Records Management Centre in your honour.

F. Burnham Gill was descended from one of Newfoundland's oldest families. An early ancestor, Captain Michael Gill, fought off a French attack on Bonavista in 1704. Michael Gill was a magistrate, merchant and a member of the Vice Admiralty court in St.

John's in the 1740's. He also had the first pew on the south entrance of the Church of England church in St. John's.

Mr. Gill was married to the former Mary Enid Saunders of Carbonear. They have two daughters, Elinor (Mrs Edward Ratcliffe) of Victoria, British Columbia and Rosalind (Mrs Peter Harris-Jones) of Toronto, Ontario.

TABLE OF CONTENTS

ACKNOWLEDGEMENTS

We wish to thank the following persons for their help in compiling this book:

The late F. Burnham Gill, J.P.
Captain Tom Goodyear
Gilbert Inkpen
David Leaman and staff of the Provincial Reference Library
Lorraine (Hynes) Louanis
Heather Wareham
Newfoundland Historical Society
Staff of the Provincial Archives

We would also like to thank Lieutenant-Governor Hon. Edward Roberts for permission to use photographs from the Estate of Dr. Harry D. Roberts. Many of these photographs previously appeared in *The Newfoundland Fish Boxes: A Chronicle of the Fishery*, by Dr. Harry D. Roberts with Michael O. Nowlan.

FOREWORD

This account of historical events describes tragedies that took place at sea during the latter part of the nineteenth century and the early days of the twentieth.

It records about thirty ships which lost the battle with the ocean, but had a somewhat happy ending in that there were one or more survivors. Unfortunately, this is only a small fraction of the total number of ships that were lost with all hands, on which information as to the circumstances is lacking.

In those days, the cod production of Newfoundland for export was largely in the form of dried salted fish and the main markets were Europe, South America and the West Indies. All of which lay far across the sea.

The mode of transportation was small wooden vessels highly dependent upon sail to reach their destination. The mariners who manned these ships were fully aware of the hazards of each voyage, but accepted the risks as a normal part of plying the trade with foreign countries.

The captain, while no doubt deep in practical knowledge and experience, had, nevertheless, little formal training, and the navigational aids were primitive by today's standards. On the other hand, there can be no question of their bravery and resourcefulness. The same applies in equal measure to the crew members.

These able seamen were a vital link in the yearly cycle of cod production and shipment abroad. They operated on behalf of the merchants in Newfoundland. They were, indeed, intrepid and without them, trade with foreign countries might never have survived.

This book is, therefore, intended as a memorial to these men and the events have been recorded so that their heroic deeds will not be forgotten.

Gilbert F. Inkpen

INTRODUCTION
Newfoundland's Foreign-Going Salt Fish Carriers

Prior to the Second World War, one of the major mainstays of the Newfoundland economy was the export of dried cod fish. Dried cod had been exported from Newfoundland since the late fifteenth century. Originally, it was carried in the ships of other nations, Basque, Spanish, French and English. This practice was maintained until about the middle of the nineteenth century, when the bulk of fish exported to foreign markets was taken over by Newfoundland carriers. With this shift in policy, thousands of Newfoundlanders began to earn their livelihood in the foreign-going salt fish trade.

Throughout the early and mid-eighteen hundreds, many of our local foreign-going vessels were built in Nova Scotia. It was not until the late 1800s that vessel construction in Newfoundland started in earnest. This was the time when many terns were built, some in the 300- to 400-ton range. During construction few outside workers were brought in and many local craftsmen who were handy at a particular trade quickly adapted themselves to the task at hand. Blacksmiths, sail makers, block makers and cordage manufacturing were all needed and played a major role in ship construction. By 1920, Newfoundland had a fleet of 150 vessels engaged in the foreign salt-fish trade.

The supply of salt cod for export came from three main sources, the Bank fishery, the Labrador fishery and the Inshore fishery.

The Bank fishery was carried on from banking schooners or bankers, whose crews fished on the various banks around Newfoundland in dories from a mother ship. The fish was split, salted and stored in the banker's hold until she returned to her home port. The fish was then dried on flakes and beaches for export to foreign markets.

The Labrador fishery was carried on by floaters and stationers from Newfoundland. The floaters were fishermen who fished from schooners from June to October or until their vessels were loaded. They then returned to their home ports to dry their catch for market. The Labrador floating fishery was carried on from earliest times. As early as 1803, there were forty-seven Newfoundland vessels with a total of 435 men fishing on the Labrador coast. The stationers were Newfoundland fishermen who took their families to the Labrador coast and fished in skiffs and punts from the many coves and bays along the coastline. Some of the stationers dried their fish on the Labrador coast before shipping it south to the Newfoundland merchants for export. Others sold their fish "green" to collectors, who would then dry the fish themselves. Some Labrador fish was exported directly to market from the Labrador coast, but the bulk was shipped south to Newfoundland ports for export. The stationery fishery dates from about 1820.

The inshore fishery was carried on from a thousand or more small fishing villages along the Newfoundland coast. Skiffs, punts and rodneys were the main type of fishing boats. Hook and line, nets, trawls and, later on, traps, were the main fishing gear of the inshore fishermen.

Over the years various methods were used in exporting the dried codfish. In early times, the fish, after processing, was stored loose in the hold of the ship. Then, the practice of shipping in drums and half drums came into use and this provided much employment for coopers around the island and especially in St. John's. In 1870, 21,600 drums of fish were exported to Pernambuco, Brazil. As the export of salt fish to overseas countries increased, foreign fish carriers were again needed and these were mostly supplied by the Norwegians and Danes, whose ships were designed as fish carriers.

There are very few personal records of day to day life on board our foreign going fish carriers and what does exist today has usually been handed down by word of mouth. We know that, by today's standards, life was rough and demanding. Every crew member had his assigned duties and was expected to carry them out. There were no eight hour days for these sailors, sea watches were maintained by the Master's decree. When off watch the crew could be called at any time to trim sail or assist in other emergencies. In order to make voyages pay, crew were kept to a minimum.

Tern schooners, it is said, were the most efficient to handle, along with being good freight carriers. A tern schooner of 200 gross tons would usually be crewed by a master, mate, cook, bosun and two seamen. A larger tern schooner would require more seamen. The crews were generally engaged in the vessel's home port, or from seamen known to the captain. This arrangement made life on board the Newfoundland ships more tolerable than on foreign flag ships where, for the most part, the crew members were unknown to each other. Therefore on the foreign ships a more rigid discipline was enforced, as the crew members would be unknown to the ship's officers.

The food on board the foreign-going vessels was rough and monotonous, but there was generally a sufficient supply if the voyage did not last too long. On the first week out of port the perishables were either used up or spoiled and canned and refrigerated foods were unheard of before World War II. Salt meat was nearly always available and was carried on deck in harness casks the name given to the containers used for that purpose. Such casks were used up to about twenty to thirty years ago on the coastal vessels. Many non-perishable foods were also carried, such as rolled oats, dried beans and lots of flour, as the cook baked fresh bread every day.

Life at sea was tough and demanding, but it held a fascination for the youth of that day, and there were many stowaways. In 1916, my father, Matthew Prim, ran away from St. Bonaventure's College in St. John's at the age of thirteen and stowed away on Crosbie's ship, *Jean,* which was bound for Pernambuco in Brazil. On the return voyage to St. John's they were intercepted by the German raider, *Thoewe.*

The *Jean* was sunk and the crew were taken as prisoners of war to Germany and interned at Hamburg. When my father's age was discovered he was repatriated by the International Red Cross and returned home.

Undeterred by this experience, he continued to go to sea and sailed for many years on sailing and steamships. He used to tell of one winter's voyage, when bound from Oporto to St. John's with a load of salt, they ran into adverse weather conditions. After two months at sea they sighted land on the Avalon Peninsula, but contrary northwest winds drove them back to the vicinity of the Azores and it was another full month before they made port in St. John's. By that time their supply of tobacco and most foodstuffs had been used up and they were reduced to smoking tea leaves and living on dried beans and water.

Sometimes, if a ship ran low on water and provisions, emergency rations would be obtained from passing ships, if the weather conditions were suitable. A winter voyage on a Newfoundland sailing ship engaged in the foreign trade on the North Atlantic was a continuous struggle for survival.

The navigational hazards faced by the captains and crews of the foreign-going vessels were many. There were sudden gales, freezing temperatures, icefields, icebergs, growlers, and the bane of all seamen, the freezing spray which could build up over a ship and cause her to founder with the loss of all her crew. In fact, many ships were lost in this way. Only people who have stood a four-hour watch exposed to winter elements on the North Atlantic can truly speak of being "blue with the cold." After coming off watch in winter it sometimes took from one to two hours to get warm enough to be able to sleep. But to stand at the wheel on an open deck in winter just above the surface of the ocean with the freezing spray coming over the vessel is an experience that no sailor today would want or be able or tolerate.

The sudden storms that blew up in the North Atlantic were a challenge to survival, especially in a vessel loaded with a cargo of salt. Salt was probably one of the most dangerous cargoes to carry in a wooden hulled ship. In a storm it could sometimes shift or get in the bilges and plug up the pumps. When this happened the crew would be on deck around the clock, manning the pumps and trying to keep them free. Sometimes the battle to save a ship could go on for weeks or even longer. All this time the crew would be without rest and proper sleep. They would be reduced to eating cold meals and be unable to dry their wet clothing. If they were in danger of foundering they waited until there was absolutely no hope of saving their vessel before abandoning her.

No vessel was ever abandoned in the North Atlantic in winter unless it was absolutely necessary. Sometimes the lifeboats and dories would be crushed or washed away in a storm and then the crew did not have the option of abandoning ship. Their only hope when this happened was to try and stay afloat until they were rescued by a passing ship. If a distressed vessel's lifeboats were destroyed or damaged, then the saving vessel would endeavour to launch her own lifeboats to make the rescue. In heavy seas and strong wind, this could be a hazardous operation. Volunteers were usually called for from the rescue vessel's crew. Many boat-crews were lost while making thse attempts in adverse weather conditions. These were the constant perils of a seaman's life in the days of sail.

Today, with all our navigational aids, we look back in amazement at the few navigational instruments available to a navigator in the days of our foreign going sailing vessels. As well, the masters and officers of the old sailing ships were not required to have certificates of competency. Some did have certificates, others had little or no instruction in the art of navigation. Who should be in command of a vessel was left to the insurance company and the owner.

However, masters were usually appointed for their sailing abilities and their knowledge of the sea. For example they could tell by instinct or colour when entering or leaving the Gulf Stream and other different types of water. They could also read the sky for signs of adverse weather.

Most of the old masters also depended on getting a noon sighting when visibility permitted. This observation required very little calculations to determine what latitude the vessel was on. To obtain an accurate position a longitude sight would also have to be taken. However, getting this sight required some complicated calculations which required the use of a chronometer. Chronometers were not usually carried in these ships and the master depended on his noon latitude sightings until he arrived at the latitude of the ship's destination. Then, the ship was sailed into port on that coordinate. This was a slow navigational process and it could take days or weeks to reach port, but usually it served its purpose.

Navigational charts were General Charts which meant the whole North Atlantic was covered on one sheet. This made all the geographical areas small and difficult to read, which was not conducive to good navigation. Accurate positioning could never be achieved on such small-scale charts. Even on vessels carrying professional navigators, sounding leads for measuring the depth of water were not carried. This, despite the fact that a knowledge of an approximate position was required, particularly when approaching the Newfoundland coast at night or in restricted visibility. Many vessels who were reported missing at sea ran ashore in isolated areas and were reduced to splinters in a matter of hours with no survivors to tell the tale.

One primary navigational aid on sailing ships was a magnetic compass which was positioned for the helmsman to steer by. The accuracy of the compass was always influenced by many conditions, and not even today can a magnetic compass be depended upon for accuracy. The other main navigational aid was the sextant or quadrant used mostly for getting a noonday sighting. The General Chart of the North Atlantic, the magnetic compass, the sextant, parallel rulers and a dividers, these were the very modest tools that were used to sail vessels halfway around the world.

The seamen who sailed these ships were men of great fortitude who suffered separation from their families. Poor food, cold and often wet living quarters, especially in winter, and the lack of any on-board entertainments or diversions to lighten the long dangerous voyage were the accepted lot of these seamen. The term "Iron Men and Wooden Ships" is certainly an appropriate one. The North Atlantic will never see their like again.

Captain Joe Prim

Men Against the Sea

ONLY ONE SURVIVOR
The Wreck of the Brig Harmony, December 9, 1869

ON DECEMBER 9, 1869, THE BRIG *HARMONY,* on a return voyage from Cadiz with a cargo of salt for the firm of Messrs. Clement & Company of Burin was off the south coast of Newfoundland. At about 8:00 P.M., that evening, the captain and most of the crew went below deck to have their supper. The only ones left on deck were those who were on watch. The weather was thick and there were snow squalls with a heavy sea running at the time.

In fact, the mate had some misgivings about their position and suggested to the captain that it might be better to "put the ship about" before they went below for supper. The captain answered "We had better have our tea first, and then we'll heave about."

They went down to tea and were about halfway through their meal when there came a heavy thump. They suspected the ship had struck a rock. The captain and the other men who were at supper rushed on deck to survey the damage. The men up top were already hoisting out the boat, just in case it should be needed. When it was hoisted out, one crewman jumped aboard, but the captain said he was staying on the ship and the other crew members said they would stick with him and remain on the ship, too.

In the meantime, the man who had jumped into the boat was cast adrift when the heavy seas broke the boat's painter. As he drifted away, someone on the brig shouted out, "There's one poor fellow lost," as the waves carried the boat toward the shore.

The boat reached the shore but was smashed to pieces on a barren rock known as Duck Island. However, the man in her managed to make it ashore on the desolate rock.

During the night the castaway could not see the *Harmony* because of the snow and the darkness. He didn't know whether or not she would survive until morning, but when dawn broke on the following day, there was no sign of the *Harmony* nor any of her crew. They had all gone down with the ship.

The position of the only survivor was now very precarious. He was only one mile from the harbour of Rose Blanche, but because of the snow squalls he could not be seen from the village. As well, the high winds and rough seas prevented the fishing skiffs from the community from going out to their fishing grounds.

For two days and nights, the sole survivor of the wreck of the *Harmony* remained without food or shelter on his rocky island. Then, on the afternoon of December 11, he saw a skiff coming his way from the opposite direction of Rose Blanche. He began to wave his arms and jump about to try and attract the attention of the men in the skiff. Luckily for him, at that moment the snow squalls slacked off a little and the men in the skiff, who were coming from Burnt Island, saw him.

They knew that he must be the survivor of a shipwreck, but, because the seas were running so high they couldn't even attempt rescue him.

Seeing the skiff go on its way without even attempting to come to his aid was a terrible disappointment to the marooned sailor. After two nights on the exposed rock with no shelter, he was fast reaching the end of his endurance and knew he wouldn't last a third night under such circumstances.

In the meantime, the Burnt Island skiff landed at Rose Blanche and raised the alarm. Immediately, a gig was manned and set out from Ridley's Island to attempt a rescue, but the men in the gig had to return empty-handed as, they couldn't risk attempting a landing. Once again the survivor of the *Harmony* despaired of rescue. The only thing in his favour was that the weather was starting to clear.

But the men of Rose Blanche did not give up easily when a fellow man was in need of rescue. When the gig returned from her failed mission, the fishermen of Rose Blanche manned their fishing skiffs and ventured out under mainsail and jib. One fisherman, a man named Jeans, at great risk to himself, put his boat close enough to Duck Island that the survivor was able to jump into her.

The rescue came none too soon, for the survivor has just about reached the limits of his endurance. His limbs were dreadfully swollen and he was nearly dead from cold, fatigue and long fasting. However, under the careful treatment of the local people he soon began to recover and tell his rescuers the story of the wreck of the *Harmony*. He was the only survivor of the shipwreck, the captain and seven other members of his crew had perished with their ship.

As soon as the weather permitted, the men of Rose Blanche attempted to find the bodies of the other crewmen. Three were located and given a decent burial. When the survivor had fully recovered he was sent back to his home.

It is remarkable that during the last week of November and the first week of December 1869, there were four wrecks in the same area of the south coast, but only in the case of the *Harmony* was there loss of life.

CAPTAIN HENRY BOWDEN'S LAST VOYAGE

The Loss of the Barque Jane Hunter, October 26, 1883

THE *JANE HUNTER,* A BARQUE belonging to Walter Grieve & Company, of St. John's was engaged in the Newfoundland foreign trade. On August 10, 1883, she cleared from the St. John's Custom House with a load of fish for Pernambuco, Brazil. This was the first load of new salt-fish to be exported from Newfoundland in 1883.

The master of the *Jane Hunter* was Captain Henry Bowden, a veteran foreign-going captain. In fact he was one of the oldest ship-masters sailing out of St. John's at that time. For years he had sailed as master of the brig *Glaucus* which was owned by J.&W. Stewart Company. Besides Captain Bowden, the *Jane Hunter's* crew included Moses Roberts, the mate, and crew members, William Seymour, Angus McDonald, Angus Wallace, William Tobin, David Taylor, Angus Rowe and Alexander Downey.

They had a good voyage to Brazil, sold their cargo and, by October 26 were near the Newfoundland coast on their return voyage. All hands were eagerly looking forward to getting home. However, because of the bad weather which had set in on October 20, Captain Bowden had been unable to verify his position with his sextant and was navigating by dead reckoning. As a result he was much closer to land than he thought.

They were making good time under full sail, but then the southeasterly winds reached gale force with heavy rain and it is likely that Captain Bowden changed his course to seek shelter in the harbour of Trepassey. A little later one of the crew members on watch saw a light and informed the captain. Because he thought they were far off land, Captain Bowden believed it to be a passing ship and kept on course for Trepassey. In the total blackness of the stormy night the *Jane Hunter* kept her course and continued on her way, her captain and crew totally unaware they were quickly driving in on land.

Around 7:00 P.M. October 26 without any warning, the *Jane Hunter* struck with terrible force on the rocks of Sheep Cove, a few miles from Trepassey. The impact tore the bottom out of the ship and huge waves began to sweep over her. It was now every man for himself as the crew members struggled for their lives.

Alexander Downey, who had been on watch up on the bow thought he could make out the faint outline of land. He jumped into the water and began to swim in that direction. The huge waves engulfed him and dragged him under, but he fought valiantly for his life. A strong swimmer, he struggled on and at last managed to make it ashore. Exhausted by his struggle, he crawled under some low bushes to get a little protection from the heavy rain. Up to this point he had not seen or heard any other of his messmates.

He lay under the bushes until, some time later, he heard a voice calling. "Is anybody saved?" It was Angus Rowe, who had managed to reach land about a quarter of a mile from where Downey had landed.

The two survivors, after they had searched in vain for any sign of their shipmates, made their way to Trepassey. Here they were welcomed and comforted by the people, who gave them food and shelter and tended to their hurts. Later they were sent on to St. John's.

A day later, searchers from Trepassey found the bodies of Captain Bowden and three of his crew who had washed up on the shore. A fifth body was found the following day.

The bodies of Captain Bowden and mate Roberts were sent to St. John's for burial, the other crew members were buried at Trepassey. Captain Bowden was a member of the Masonic Order and his funeral took place from the Masonic Temple to the Anglican Cemetery in St. John's, where Reverend A. Heygate, the senior curate at the Anglican Cathedral, officiated. A large number of friends and brother Masons attended his funeral.

The southeasterly gale which had helped bring about the wreck of the *Jane Hunter* devastated shipping in many other areas around the Newfoundland coast.

One of the indirect results of the tragedy of the *Jane Hunter* was the erection of a light on Powell's Head, Trepassey. For a number of years many sea captains and ship-owners as well as the people of Trepassey had been petitioning the Newfoundland Government to put a light on Powell's Head. The tragedy of the *Jane Hunter* helped reinforce their arguments and in 1902 a light was erected.

ADRIFT IN THE NORTH ATLANTIC

The Schooner Maranee Abandoned
April 6, 1885

ON THE AFTERNOON OF Thursday, April 23, 1885, the lookout on the Brig *Seretha* saw a small boat on the lee bow. He reported this to the captain, who ordered his vessel to go alongside the boat. In it they found part of the crew of the Newfoundland schooner, *Maranee*, owned by A. Goodridge & Son of St. John's and skippered by Captain Sol Bowden. An entry in the logbook for April 23, 1885, by Captain Jeremiah Callahan of the *Seretha* reads:

> Thursday, the 23rd of April, 2:00 P.M. Saw a small boat on the lee bow. Kept ship away and got boat alongside. Found it contained the captain and crew of the *Maranee* 113 days out from Figueria. They were taken on board and made comfortable. They were very weak and had suffered terribly.

The *Maranee* had left St. John's late in December with a load of fish for Portugal. The 158-ton barquentine had made many an Atlantic crossing. They had a pleasant and uneventful voyage to Portugal, where they discharged their fish and took on a cargo of 160 tons of salt for A. Goodridge & Son.

On New Year's Day, 1885, they set sail from the port of Figueira de Foz for St. John's. The weather remained good until they passed the Azores and Captain Bowden hoped for a quick passage home. However, the North Atlantic can be cruel in winter, and just after passing the Azores they ran into adverse westerly head winds which soon developed into a violent winter storm. The winds grew to hurricane force and ripped the sails from the *Maranee.* At the same time huge waves smashed the schooner's bulwarks. Totally disabled, the stricken ship wallowed helplessly in the waves that threatened to engulf her. For three weeks the vessel was tossed around, and the terrified crew were afraid each moment might be their last. All this time the ship was drifting toward Newfoundland, but on February 17, she entered a field of ice which held her fast.

The *Maranee* remained stuck in the ice until March 6, when the ice around her began to raft. The crushing ice cut through the ship's bow planking on both sides and water began to pour into her. Captain Bowden immediately ordered his men to trim the cargo aft and bring the ship's bow out of water. Then, using tarred canvas and sheets of copper the crew made repairs and kept the vessel afloat. They also jettisoned thirty-five tons of salt. Five days later they dumped another thitry-five tons of cargo. For the next month, the now totally disabled *Maranee* drifted with the ice pack, somehow keeping afloat, despite a number of violent storms that swept over the area.

On March 20, the winds and waves abated somewhat, and again the crew tried to patch the damaged areas by stuffing more canvas into the holes cut by the ice. However, the fine weather did not hold, and soon it was again stormy and the pressure of the ice began to crack the ship's timbers.

Matters continued like this until April 6, when, with two feet of water in the holds, and still rising, despite the constant pumping, it became clear that the vessel was rapidly sinking. A reluctant Captain Bowden finally gave the order to abandon ship. They had two boats, a longboat and a smaller jollyboat. Captain Bowden took command of the jollyboat and William Sheaves, the cook, and William Adams, the bosun went with him. The *Maranee's* mate, Pat Davis, took command of the larger longboat and the other four crew members, Pat MacDonald, Michael Edstrom, Richard Coady and James Cane went with him. The two boats pulled away from the rapidly sinking *Maranee,* became separated, and the longboat and its crew were never seen again.

The jollyboat became stuck in the ice near the mother ship and Captain Bowden and his men had to pull her up on the ice. They were there for thirty-six hours and nearly froze to death. It became so cold the captain had to burn his log book and charts to try and keep warm. The next day the *Maranee* sank and they got some drift wood from the wreck to make a fire.

After getting their boat back in the water, Captain Bowden and his men sailed and rowed among the ice floes. They had hail and rain and snow, and several times the ice damaged their little craft. Each time this happened, they had to pull her up on the ice and make repairs as best they could. It was only the indomitable spirit and courage of the sixty-year-old Captain Bowden that kept them going.

On the eighth day after they had abandoned ship, Sheaves, the cook, gave up hope of rescue and felt he would die before nightfall. He begged Captain Bowden not to bury him at sea. However, Captain Bowden soon persuaded the cook that help was near, and Sheaves recovered from his despair and was again able to take a turn at steering the boat.

On April 22, a violent storm came up and mountainous waves threatened to engulf the little craft and her half-starved, half-frozen crew. The boat filled with water and the men had to bail constantly to keep her free. Loose ice now became a great danger, as the wind and waves tossed the jollyboat around. The men in the jollyboat now lost their food supply, as their bread became salt-water soaked and useless.

Things were getting really desperate. A gale blew from the northwest and the ice surrounding the jollyboat began to break up. The small boat was buried in swells that half-filled the little craft and Captain Bowden and Adams had to bail constantly while Sheaves did his best to keep her head on to the waves. When day dawned on the twenty-third of April, Captain Bowden and his men were in desperate condition, and it seemed only a matter of hours before they would have to give up their fight for survival and lie down and die. Then to their joy, they saw the *Seretha* coming towards them, her white sails billowing in the wind. In a short time they were on board their rescue ship, being tended with the best of care. Later his men paid tribute to their captain for his relentless fight to bring them to safety.

COLLISION WITH AN ICEBERG

The Loss of the Barquentine Susan, March 26, 1887

ON FRIDAY MORNING, March 25, 1887, the barquentine *Susan,* under the command of Captain Michael Ryan, left St. John's with a load of fish for the West Indies. The ship carried a crew of seven. On leaving port they made slow headway, the wind being contrary. As well, the drifting pans of ice were numerous and the *Susan* was brought up suddenly several times by closely packed pans.

The winds and ice made for slow going, but by noon on Saturday, March 26, the *Susan* was finally in clear water and tacking to and fro off Cape Broyle. The only obstacle remaining in her path was an iceberg of large proportions. The weather was clear and the iceberg was plainly visible to the captain and crew.

The wind was southwest and the men on the *Susan* were sure that they were sufficiently to windward of the iceberg to avoid it. However, as the ship approached the giant iceberg, she suddenly made way so rapidly and unexpectedly, that before the crew could take evasive action she was within two hundred and fifty yards of the iceberg. It was now necessary, in order to escape collision, that the Susan should fall off to leeward, and they still had time to do this.

However, when this manoeuvre was tried, the main sails didn't work and this, in part, caused the disaster that followed. Unknown to the captain and crew, the halyards were frozen in their blocks, and neither the mainsail nor spanker could be lowered in time to let the ship fall clear of the iceberg. They cleared the main body of the berg but then struck the end of it with such tremendous force that it smashed the ship's head works and stove in her bow.

After the collision, the *Susan* drifted clear of the iceberg, but she was now a helpless wreck, with the ocean pouring in through the gaping hole in her bow threatening to sink her at any moment.

Realizing that the ship was doomed, Captain Ryan and his crew made hasty preparations to abandon her. The *Susan's* small boat was available, but Captain Ryan was determined to use the larger boat and, with the help of John Lahey and Walter Walsh, the bosun, tried to launch her, but the larger boat proved too heavy and they could not get her over the side. The other crew members, trying to gather their clothes and belongings, did not come to the aid of the captain and his helpers.

In half an hour the vessel settled down in the water, but did not sink immediately. The large boat now floated free and John Lahey, Walter Walsh and Frank Dillon all managed to get into her. Seeing that Captain Ryan was clinging to the rigging, they shoved the boat towards him. At first he would not quit his hold on the rigging, but at last was prevailed upon to get in the boat, which was now caught between the main and mizzen-masts. In trying to push her clear she tangled in the jump-stay and upset, throwing Captain Ryan and the other three men into the icy water. The last that John Lahey, one of the survivors, saw of Captain Ryan he was being held up in the water by his cork life preserver. Lahey, while in the water, seized one of the boat chock's that had floated free and kept himself afloat after the *Susan* sank. Walter Walsh, another survivor clung to a ladder. The waves from the iceberg washed over them and they went under, just managing to surface long enough to draw a breath before they were again pushed under.

Three other crew members, John Bayley, Thomas Mallard and Frank Dillon managed to upright the boat after she turned over, although it was filled with water. She overturned again and two of the men, Thomas Mallard and Frank Dillon fell out of her. John Bayley clung to the stern.

In the meantime, Captain Joy, of the schooner *Muriel* from Carbonear, saw what had happened and hastened to the rescue of the *Susan's* crew. Within ten minutes the survivors, John Lahey, Walter Walsh and John Bayley, a native of Australia, were plucked from the ocean. Captain Michael Ryan, mate John Gall, seaman Frank Dillon, all Newfoundlanders, and seaman John Allen and steward Thomas Mallard, from abroad, were all lost.

The three survivors from the wreck of the *Susan* were in shock and suffering from exposure when they were taken on board the *Muriel*. Captain Joy immediately had them served warm wine and wrapped them in warm blankets in a bed. He then changed his course to take the men back to St. John's. However, in Freshwater Bay he encountered the SS *Hercules* and she took the survivors in to St. John's.

The survivors were landed in St. John's at 7:00 P.M. on Saturday evening, March 26, with great praise for Captain Joy and his men. They said that it was only the speed with which they were rescued that had saved their lives, as they could not have held on much longer in the icy water.

The men lost everything in the shipwreck, but hoped they would get some help from the Government Fund for Shipwrecked Sailors.

TWO WRECKS AT THE DEVIL'S CHIMNEY

The Corisande, 1894, and the Helen Isabel, 1904

IN THE FALL OF 1893, BOB BARTLETT, an eighteen-year-old Labrador skipper, decided he wanted to sail in the foreign trade. He approached Captain Hughes, the master of the barquentine, *Corisande* for a berth. Captain Hughes asked him a few questions and then told him to go to Baine Johnson & Company's shipping office and sign articles.

The *Corisande* was engaged in the foreign trade and Bob Bartlett signed on as ordinary seaman before the mast. A few days later they left St. John's with a load of dried fish for Pernambuco, Brazil. The other sailors on the barquentine told Bartlett the usual run to Pernambuco took thirty days. On this voyage she took sixty-nine days and there were omens of disaster.

First, there was the fight on the deck of the *Corisande* before they had cleared the Narrows, with one man knocked unconscious by another seaman. Then there was an uneasy atmosphere, with much bickering among the ship's company. The ship's cat disappeared mysteriously, and sometimes it seemed to Bob Bartlett that the ship trembled from stem to stern for no reason at all. The men complained of the salt beef and the cook and captain had a terrible row. Bob's watchmate got hit over the eye and Bob had to do double-wheel tricks. Then Bob got a boil on his neck that turned to a carbuncle. Captain Hughes wanted to lance the carbuncle, but Bartlett was afraid to let him at it. The cook cured it with hot barley poultices.

However, despite Bob Bartlett's premonitions of disaster, they finally made it to Pernambuco. As there was no return freight, they left for St. John's in ballast. Now the *Corisande* made up for the slowness of her outward voyage. They had good weather and the ship seemed to be racing for home. They reached Cape Cod and experienced cold weather, with snow flurries. From here the skipper laid his course for Cape Race, Newfoundland.

By this time Captain Hughes wasn't on speaking terms with the mate, and when the old ship was tearing along under full sail, making a good ten knots, the mate felt this was too much strain on the vessel, but could voice no objection to the skipper. Then, when they were nearing the Newfoundland coast, the wind picked up, and the heavy seas caused the *Corisande* to stick her bowsprit clear under the waves. The ship was also beginning to ice up, and two crew members were detailed to chop the ice off her standing rigging. The old ship was suffering under the strain of too many sails and it appeared the mate was right, for she began to leak, as some of her seams were pulled apart.

Then, just as dawn was breaking, the *Corisande* struck at a place known to seamen as the Devil's Chimney, the most dangerous spot on the Southern Shore. Sheer cliffs, three times the height of the ship's masts, towered over the wrecked vessel. Luckily, at the time they struck there was a lull in the storm. During this lull the crew got the boats over the side and they rowed in toward the cliffs. looking for a landing place. There was no time to lose. for the storm began picking up again, with the wind from the northwest and the surf getting stronger. Just in time, they found a narrow opening in the cliffs with a small sand spit. A big wave hit them and the boat was swamped, but they all got safely ashore.

From this vantage point, Bob Bartlett watched the angry wind and waves tear the *Corisande* apart and, in a few minutes nothing of the ship was left above water. Finally, one of the seamen managed to climb up the face of the cliff and made it to a fishermen's shack, where a number of men were weathering out the storm. They came back with ropes and hauled the rest of the crew to safety. All hands were saved.

Despite this harrowing experience on his first voyage in the foreign trade, Bob Bartlett went on to become Newfoundland's most famous master mariner and Arctic explorer.

THE WRECK OF THE HELEN ISABEL

On May 18, 1904, Baine Johnson & Company lost another ship, the *Helen Isabel,* to the Devil's Chimney. In fact, she came to rest on the other side of the giant boulder where the *Corisande* had found her last resting place some ten years earlier

The *Helen Isabel* was a 267-ton barque engaged in the foreign trade. She had been launched at Greenock in August of 1867 and was thirty-seven years old at the time she was lost. She was one of the best-known vessels in the Newfoundland foreign trade.

On her last voyage, the *Helen Isabel,* under the command of Captain William Lawrie, left Pernambuco, Brazil, on April 4, 1904, for Barbados. After a record ten-day run she arrived there, where she loaded 515 puncheons and 400 barrels of molasses for Baine

Johnson & Company of St. John's. On April 29, she set sail from Barbados for St. John's.

The *Helen Isabel* struck splendid weather on her return voyage to Newfoundland and this held all the way up the Atlantic seaboard. Then, with Cape Race bearing 150 miles northeast by east and a fresh south-south-west wind, the fog settled down and enshrouded the ship, so that, from the taffrail a man could scarcely be seen on the lookout.

Under light topsails and a good spread of lower canvas the *Helen Isabel* made excellent time, and the captain had made allowance for the insetting tides, which were known as a navigational hazard around the Cape Race area. Occasionally they heard the whistles of steamships passing east and west from the St. Lawrence, but no one suspected that the insetting tide was dragging them closer and closer to the treacherous rocks .

At about 10:00 A.M. on May 18, 1904, they heard the sound of a steam whistle passing inside the *Helen Isabel* and felt quite safe. Fifteen minutes later, they crashed into a small cove one mile west of Mistaken Point. The bottom of the *Helen Isabel* was torn out and she came to rest at the base of the Devil's Chimney, where the *Corisande* had met her fate ten years earlier. The vessel began to fill rapidly and it was clear the eleven man crew and two passengers had only minutes to take to the lifeboat. One sailor panicked and ran to the jib-boom with the intention of jumping for the cliff. He was pulled back from what would have been certain death by his messmates.

They had no time to collect their personal belongings, for the vessel was settling fast. Acting quickly, they had the lifeboat launched in five minutes and the crew put off from the rapidly sinking ship. Captain Lawrie had only time to grab the ship's strong box, which was on a locker in his cabin, but lost all his personal effects, including his watch and nautical instruments. They had only rowed a little distance from their ship which was lying against a huge boulder, when she slipped beneath the waves. From the time she struck until she went to the bottom just twelve minutes had elapsed.

Captain Lawrie now took command of the lifeboat and they rowed along the shore until they came to Biscay Cove, where they landed. They stayed there until the next morning and then rowed on to Cape Race. Here they were taken in and looked after by Mr. Myrick, the lighthouse keeper. Captain Lawrie and his crew were loud in their praise of the kindness shown them by Mr. Myrick and his family, who did everything in their power to make the shipwrecked crew comfortable.

The survivors of the ill fated *Helen Isabel included* Joe Benson and Martret Aguste, two sailors from the *Gladioli* which had been lost earlier. Arrangements were made to take Captain Lawrie and his crew back to their homes where they were welcomed by their families.

None of the cargo from the *Helen Isabel* was salvaged for, as the bungs were out of the casks for the voyage to St. John's the molasses was all spoiled by the salt water.

By a strange twist of fate. two ships from Baine Johnson & Company came to rest not twenty yards from each other within the same decade.

A CUCKOLD'S COVE SHIPWRECK

The Loss of the Barquentine Stella, January 17, 1904

THE *STELLA* WAS A 234-ton wooden barquentine built in 1872. She was 121 feet, seven inches long, twenty-five feet, eight inches wide and thirteen feet deep. In 1904, the thirty-two-year-old ship was being used by Baird Gordon Company in the foreign trade.

Around six o'clock on the evening of January 17, 1904, Hans Jensen, a sailor from the barquentine *Stella,* reported to the Baird Gordon's watchman at Baird's Cove that the *Stella,* under the command of Captain Jones, had gone ashore at Cuckold's Cove near Quidi Vidi. He had been sent in to St. John's to ask that a tug be sent to her assistance.

The watchman immediately contacted Mr. H. Baird, and the tug *John Green* was sent, with a number of employees of Baird Gordon, to help the crew of the stranded ship. The tug returned around 9:00 P.M. and reported that they found no sign of the vessel, and the heavy seas running in the area prevented them from entering very far into Cuckold's Cove to make a search for any survivors.

On the return of the *John Green* from Cuckold's Cove, a rumour spread about St. John's that the *Stella* had been lost, with eight of her crew missing. Immediately, the relatives of the missing crew members made their way to Baird Gordon's wharf to ask for information. However, soon after the tug's return, Murphy, another seaman from the *Stella* reached town to say that the barquentine was gone, but the captain and all the crew members of the *Stella* had made it safely to shore. On hearing this news a number of men set out by land for Cuckold's Cove to render assistance to the shipwrecked crew. A detachment of policemen were also dispatched to safeguard any salvage from the wreck.

The mate of the *Stella,* Mr. Martin, later told the story of the last voyage of the barquentine.

They had carried a load of fish to Pernambuco and, on December 22, 1903 had left that South American port for St. John's. They had a good run up the North American seaboard, and about 3:15 on the evening of January 17, 1904 could see Cape Spear quite plainly. They then decided to run for the Narrows. The wind was about southeast, quite strong and accompanied by snow squalls. They shaped their course for the Narrows and the snow squalls became less thick. But then, the wind suddenly increased and a heavy snow squall obscured visibility. Despite the zero visibility, they decided that they were right on course for the Narrows and kept their way. Then, around 4:00 P.M., without warning, the cliffs of Cuckold's Cove Head suddenly loomed out of the snow directly ahead of them and they were only a few feet from the rocks.

Immediately, they tried to bring the vessel around, but with so little seaway this was an impossible task and she went ashore, striking the cliffs, which tore away all her headgear and cracked the bowsprit. The ship finally grounded on a rock and shivered from stem to stern with the contact.

As soon as she struck it was apparent that the crew would have no difficulty in getting ashore if they had to abandon ship. There was, however, some danger that her spars might come down and crush some of them on the deck. The ship had been under lower and upper topsail and one staysail when she struck.

After the initial shock of striking, the captain ordered the manning of the pumps. They were sounded and it was apparent that the *Stella* was leaking badly and, with the pounding of the ship against the rocks would soon be a total wreck. The men then quickly gathered up their clothes and personal belongings and, in good order left the ship to take shelter on the cliffs that towered above them. The captain was the last man to leave the vessel. Had they run ashore after dark, the mate was sure they might have had some difficulty in landing and perhaps lost some of the crew.

Captain Jones remained in Cuckold's Cove during the night of January 17 and the owners hoped that a tug might tow the vessel off when the seas abated. However, she was filled with water when Captain Jones left her, and he did not feel that the hull could be salvaged.

Besides Captain R. Jones, master, the crew consisted of mate, William Martin, bosun, Richard Wakeham, cook, John Lamb, and seamen Thomas Edstrom, Joseph

Murphy, P. Lundrigan, Stephen Smolkham and Hans Jensen.

By a strange coincidence, another ship, the *Corsair* was lost in the same place on December 5, 1865, again, with no loss of life.

CHRISTMAS ON A RESCUE SHIP

The Loss of the Barquentine, Blanch, December 22, 1905

AT 10:00 A.M. ON DECEMBER 7, 1904, the barquentine *Blanch*, owned by Job Brothers & Company of St. John's, set sail from that port under the command of Captain William Sinclair. The ship carried a cargo of dry fish packed in drums for the Brazilian market.

As the ship sailed out through the Narrows the wind was from the northwest and there was a heavy sea. The next day the weather remained rather stormy, and in the evening the wind swung around to the southeast and was accompanied by snow. Then, as the ship neared Cape Race, the wind switched around again to the south southwest and Captain Sinclair had to shorten sail. On the evening of December 8, they rounded Cape Race under close hauled canvas.

On December 9, around 10:00 A.M., the wind changed again. It now became squally and, by evening reached hurricane force, with the seas running mountainously high. The vessel wallowed in huge waves that threatened to engulf her. Late in the evening the foresail burst and the ship was put under small reaching canvas.

The next day, December 10, the storm increased in violence and heavy waves swept over the vessel, filling her decks. Later, toward nightfall, a comber struck the unfortunate vessel and burst the mizzen. A few minutes later the wind tore the foretop staysail to ribbons. Around 8:00 P.M. another giant wave filled the mainsail, and it too, burst into pieces.

All that night the gale raged and the ship could not carry an inch of canvas, but drifted helplessly with the wind and waves. The storm continued on Monday, with the winds even more violent than before. As well, there was a hard frost and the ship iced-up, which made it very dangerous.

The weather continued stormy until the next Tuesday, when there came a lull in the gale-force winds. During this, The crew were able to cut the tattered sails from their flapping laces and bend new ones. This gave the schooner steerage way. The wind then changed to the west and remained light for several days, which allowed the crew to clear away some of the wreckage from the storm. Then the wind changed again to the northwest and reached gale force before morning. The new mainsail was torn from the mast. This time, scraps of the old sails had to be sewn together and used wherever possible to keep the schooner to the wind.

The evening of Wednesday, December 17, closed in with a wild looking horizon and the barometer standing at 28.20. It looked like another storm was on its way. The waves were still so high that they were threatening to engulf the schooner, but somehow she managed to stay afloat. Then, the storm arrived with hurricane force and the crew had never experienced anything like it. At 2:00 A.M. a sudden squall threw the *Blanch* on her beam end, and the captain and crew feared it was all over. The ship lay in this position until six o'clock the next morning when the captain ordered the foremast to be cut away. This, under the circumstances, was a dangerous job, and the mate had to stand waist deep in water to carry out the command. The falling foremast carried the main topmast and jib-boom with it and this eased the strain on the ship and she up-righted herself.

Now the *Blanch* was only a ravished hull, rising and falling with the swells. As well, all the head gear now being gone, the vessel wallowed in the heavy seas and every wave that broke over her threatened to tear the stern completely out of her. Luckily, the sea began to abate and the crew cut through the deck of the cabin which was filled with water, and 300 casks of fish were floated up on deck and jettisoned to try and stabilize the ship.

The plan worked, but around midnight, the wind which had moderated, began to increase, and rain fell in torrents. On the nineteenth the wind changed to the west again and seas swept over the decks, taking away the broken lifeboat.

In the early morning of December 20, the gale from the west sprung up again and the decks became flooded. It was now found necessary to jettison another 300 casks of fish. While the crew were getting the fish from the hold, they discovered that the cargo had shifted and the *Blanch* was leaking badly.

It was now clear that it was only a matter of time before the ship would sink. Realizing the danger, Captain Sinclair ordered the crew to rig a jib and other pieces of sail to try and reach the major sea lanes where they might be rescued.

On December 21, there was another strong breeze and, with her tattered pieces of sail set, the *Blanch* made good time. On December 22, they sighted a steamer and sent up distress signals. The vessel proved to be the Swedish steamer, SS *Seveland,* Captain J. Christianson, bound from Savannah with a load of cotton for Bremen via Norfolk.

On reading their distress signals a boat was launched from the SS *Seveland* and took off Captain Sinclair and crew. Before leaving the *Blanch,* they removed her hatches to let her sink, so that she would not become a danger to shipping. This was in latitude 42 degrees 36 minutes and longitude 41 degrees 14 minutes.

The SS *Seveland* had a stormy nine day trip and Captain Sinclair and his crew celebrated Christmas Day with their rescuers. Christmas was celebrated in fine style on the *Seveland,* but the Newfoundlanders sadly remembered happier Christmas celebrations at home. They longed for the sweetbread and other goodies that had always marked the occasion.

On December 30 the *Seveland* was off Dungeness, England and a steam pilot cutter came alongside. Her captain was asked to take the shipwrecked Newfoundland crew ashore. He wanted one pound per man to do this. Captain Christianson was enraged at such treatment of a shipwrecked crew and he and the pilot boat captain had bitter words over the matter. It ended with Captain Christianson going into port and landing the men himself.

When Captain Sinclair and his crew landed they had more difficulty. The Dungeness Board of Trade refused to help them because their shipping articles said they were to be paid off in Liverpool. Finally, the Liverpool Shipwrecked Mariners Society took charge of the men and sent them to Liverpool. They arrived in Liverpool on New Year's Day and left for home on January 3, 1905. They arrived safely and, undaunted by their terrible experience were soon at sea again.

THIRTY-THREE DAYS IN A LIFEBOAT

The Loss of the Electra, April 26, 1909

ON MAY 29, 1909, about eight o'clock in the evening, a number of people on the St. John's waterfront saw a lifeboat come through the Narrows and row up to Goodridge's wharf. The watchers were curious as to where the lifeboat had come from. Some said the boat belonged to the *Electra,* a schooner owned by Alan Goodridge & Sons, which was due on a return voyage from Oporto. As the boat drew nearer some of the men recognized Captain Cave, who had sailed as master of the *Electra*. Most of the men rushed to Goodridge's wharf to find out what had happened.

When the lifeboat had docked, Captain Cave climbed up on the wharf, shook hands with a few friends, and told them the *Electra* was lost, but all of the crew were safe in the lifeboat. Later, at his home on Leslie Street, Captain Cave told the story of the last voyage of the *Electra*.

They left Oporto on March 23, 1909 with a full load of salt for Alan Goodyear & Sons. The first week at sea was uneventful and they hoped for a smooth crossing. The ship did run a little short of freshwater, but a passing German steamer refilled their water tanks. Then, shortly after their meeting with the German steamer, the weather changed and a series of gales swept the ocean. So changeable were the winds that the *Electra* was three times blown back to her position at the start of the storms.

These storms were so fierce that the waves rolled mountainously high, smashed the bulwarks and did some other minor damage to the vessel. At one time the gale raged so fiercely that the *Electra* was hove to for eighty-five hours, trying to ride out the storm. During this time drags and oil bags were put out to try and keep the vessel up to the wind and keep her from drifting too much to the leeward. This same storm swept away a small dog that the captain was bringing back from Oporto to his daughter.

Despite the bad weather, the *Electra* made progress, but on Wednesday, the twenty-first of April at 2:30 P.M., they encountered ice. By mid-afternoon they were into heavy ice and jammed so badly that the stern and bow sections became twisted and water started to pour into the ship. The pumps were manned, but to no avail; they could not clear the ship.

As part of her return cargo the *Electra* carried twenty puncheons of wine and one of the crew was sent to the hold to smash the heads of the puncheons so the wine could be pumped overboard. For a little while the crew pumped wine and water out of the sinking ship, but as the pumps were unable to clear the ship, Captain Cave gave the order to prepare two lifeboats for a long sea voyage.

While some of the crew provisioned the two boats and gathered their personal belongings, the remainder stayed at the pumps, to keep the *Electra* afloat until they were ready to leave her. However, she was leaking so badly that, shortly after the captain and crew had abandoned her, she plunged headfirst to the bottom.

The men in the lifeboat were Captain Cave, first mate, Bert Cave, the captain's son, boatswain, Ambrose King, cook, Martin Billard, and seamen Tom Croucher, Thomas Philpott, John Dazzle, a coloured man, and Alexander Wentzel, a native of Belgium. All hands were in one lifeboat because it was discovered that the second boat had a leak and the hole had been covered with canvas. However, Captain Cave decided to tow the second boat astern, as he feared she might be needed later on.

Once the *Electra* had disappeared beneath the sea, Captain Cave took the tiller and set his course for St. John's. The crew manned the oars and they began the long trek through the ice-infested waters. The men worked bravely and, every so often, Captain Cave, hummed a sailor's ditty to encourage them. He also set up a system so that the crew would, in their turn, have an hour or two of rest by lying in the bottom of the boat. Captain Cave and his son, Bert took turns at the tiller, and both men showed great leadership in keeping up the spirits of the crew. They had to row through a good deal of slob ice, and this slowed their progress, but once in open water they made good time.

The *Electra* had been well provisioned, and Captain Cave had made sure they took sufficient food to keep them going. He was loud in his praise of Alan Goodridge & Sons for the food supplies issued to the *Electra,* saying the ship carried enough supplies to last for a six month voyage. The only thing they missed was having a hot drink. This was impossible, as they had no way of making a fire in the lifeboat. As the days grew into weeks, two of the men became delirious for a short time, but under the encouragement of Captain Cave they soon recovered.

They had hoped to fall in with a ship, but for the thirty-three-day voyage in the lifeboat not a sail was sighted until they were entering the Narrows. The only consolation they had was that a large number of seabirds followed the boat, which indicated that they were approaching land.

Captain Cave was no stranger to shipwrecks. During his forty-seven years at sea he had experienced shipwreck off the coast of China and spent eighteen days in an open boat. He was later shipwrecked in the Persian Gulf and also off the coast of Brazil. It was his great experience in such disasters that helped him bring his crew to safety.

In 1958, a local newspaper told the story of the loss of the *Electra* and interviewed Thomas Croucher, who had been a sailor on the ship. His greatest memory of the event was the joy of being able to get a hot drink when he landed. He told the reporter:

> As I got ashore I was met by an old friend James Murphy who worked for the City Council, and a few of us were taken up to Strang's for a good hot drink with lemon and sugar.

He went on to lament the fact that now there were no hot drinks, nothing only beer parlours, and you got chilled drinking cold beer.

IN SIGHT OF THE NARROWS

The Wreck of the Geisha, June 6, 1909

ON MAY 12, 1909, the 130-ton schooner *Geisha,* under command of Captain Enon left Cadiz, Spain, for Newfoundland. The *Geisha* had been built at Appledore, Nova Scotia, in 1906 for R. Cook and Sons, who employed her in the foreign trade.

The ship had a good voyage for the first few days, with favourable winds and calm seas. Then, when they were about 150 miles east of the Grand Banks, they encountered icebergs. On Thursday, June 1, they had their first misfortune, when they rammed an iceberg, which carried away the *Geisha's* bowsprit, and all her top canvas. It took some time to get the wreckage cleared away and her sails back in place.

That same night there was more trouble. The *Geisha* ran into another schooner, which had no sidelights up. Captain Enon called out to know the name of the ship they had struck. A voice answered the *William Bearns* and without any further information, the ship disappeared into the night. It was later discovered that there was no such ship in either the Newfoundland coastal or foreign trade. Captain Enon thought that *William Bearns* might be the captain's name and not that of the ship, but nothing further was ever heard of her.

After these two accidents the voyage proceeded smoothly until June 6 around 10:30 P.M., when they were about two miles to the eastward of Cape Spear, they discovered there was a large iceberg in the immediate area and the tide was carrying the *Geisha* toward it. There was nothing that Captain Enon and his crew could do but stand and watch their ship being carried closer to the berg. When it became evident to all hands that a collision with the berg was unavoidable, Captain Enon ordered his men to take to the lifeboats, which they did in an orderly fashion.

They had only rowed about fifty metres from the ship when the *Geisha* struck the iceberg. It immediately tumbled over and sunk the vessel. It was good seamanship on Captain Enon's part, that he had seen the danger in time to save his crew. With the ship gone, the crew manned the oars and began to row towards the Narrows. They had only rowed about half the distance when a passing schooner, the *Jessie B,* commanded by Captain Parsons of Greenspond, took them on board, and they reached St. John's about 7:00 A.M.

The captain and crew had to take to the lifeboat so suddenly that they hadn't even had time to get their clothes. This loss was keenly felt by the crew members, who lost all their personal belongings. The captain and crew were all Englishmen with the sole exception of one crew member, who was from Trinity, Newfoundland.

A GENEROUS NORWEGIAN CAPTAIN

The Wreck of the Aureola, January 27, 1912

ON NOVEMBER 22, 1911, the 288-ton barquentine *Aureola,* owned by Bishop Sons & Company of St. John's, left Troon, Scotland with a load of coal for St. John's. The vessel was under the command of Captain Christopher Olsen and carried a crew of nine men and one passenger, a boy named McKinley. The voyage started off well, but on November 27 they ran into a terrible storm.

The *Aureola* was a stout vessel and she had been fitted out with the best Glasgow canvas before leaving Scotland. However, the fury of the northwest gale, which raged for twenty-six hours, split the mainsail, and Captain Olsen and his crew had to repair the sails as best they could. But the storm, instead of abating sprang up again and, on December 12, carried away part of their foresail.

Again they repaired the damage, but by December 20, the storm raged with such violence that they could not set an inch of canvas, and had to lay to under bare poles on the starboard tack. The seas were now breaking over the decks of the battered barquentine, and for a day and a half she was practically under water.

On December 21, Captain Olsen had a narrow escape from death when a sea swept in under the lower topsail and knocked him flat on the deck. Half-stunned by the fall, Captain Olsen had the presence of mind to grab hold of the mizzen sheet and kept himself from being washed overboard. However, the captain injured his right side in the fall, and in great pain, had to go below.

In the meantime, about 8:00 P.M., such a tremendous sea was running, the vessel had to heave to again and try to ride out the storm. By midnight the strain on the ship was beginning to tell and, as she laboured and strained in that monstrous sea, it seemed impossible that she could survive. In describing that awful night, Captain Olsen later said he had been at sea for twenty-eight years, having first sailed as a boy of fifteen, but had never witnessed such a storm.

It was a miserable Christmas Day for the captain and crew of the *Aureola,* for they did not know at what minute their vessel might founder. All through the later days of December there was one storm after another, and the ship was constantly battered by wind and waves, with no let-up. However, despite the battering, the *Aureola* still kept afloat. Then, on January 5, 1912, their position became critical.

At about 4:00 A.M. January 5, the barquentine was lying-to on the starboard tack and labouring in the heavy seas. Around 6:00 A.M. she shipped a heavy sea, which carried away the stanchions, bulwarks, rails, backstays and boats on the starboard side. At the same time, the vessel sprung a leak and the crew had to man the pumps. It was now evident to all hands that they were in a very dangerous position, and they worked hard to keep the leaking *Aureola* afloat.

The storm abated a little during the next four days giving a little hope to Captain Olsen and his men, but on January 9 there was another violent Atlantic gale from the southwest. Just after midnight on January 10, a huge sea swept over the deck of the battered *Aureola,* sweeping everything that was moveable overboard. The vessel was now a total wreck, and the captain took what measures he could to keep her afloat until they sighted another vessel.

The crew were divided up into pumping gangs who relieved each other every two hours, and they tried to lighten the ship by throwing large quantities of her cargo overboard. To add to their danger the ship's cargo shifted, and to keep her from rolling over the masts had to be cut away. This was done at great danger to the crew because of the falling wreckage.

In this desperate situation all hands knew the only way to escape death was to keep the *Aureola* afloat until a passing ship took them off the derelict barquentine. Desperately and persistently, the men kept pumping. The waves kept sweeping over the deck of the vessel and the sound of the gale struck terror into the hearts of the desperate men. Then came a spark of hope, they sighted a ship and sent up their distress signals. The ship ignored their signals and kept on her way. Another ship was sighted but again, she did not come to the aid of the stricken vessel.

It would be impossible to describe the emotions of the crew of the sinking *Aureola* as they witnessed ship after ship, five in all, refuse to give assistance. According to Captain Olsen, one of the passing ships was so close they could see the men on her bridge, but they made no attempt to come to the rescue of the crew of the sinking ship.

As the days passed with no help from the passing ships the spirits of the crew fell, but with dogged determination they manned the pumps and kept their vessel afloat. Then, on January 27, their luck changed when a Norwegian ship, the SS *Marle*, under the command of Captain Monsen, saw their distress signals and came alongside.

The seas were still running high and the men from the *Marle* had great difficulty in launching a lifeboat, but finally succeeded and, in two trips, took Captain Olsen, his crew and passenger on board. Before leaving the *Aureola*, Captain Olsen set fire to her, as she was now a navigational hazard. Afterwards, the fire from the burning ship could be seen twenty miles away.

The captain and crew of the SS *Marle* gave every assistance they could to the exhausted crew of the *Aureola* and on their arrival in London the men were sent to the Sailors Home where, once again, they were treated with every kindness.

In an interview with a St. John's newspaper, Captain Olsen was quoted as saying: "It was a terrible experience and I hope I may never have to face the same again."

JOHN FOOTE, A YOUNG BELLEORAM HERO

The Loss of the Schooner John Harvey, January 10, 1912

THE *JOHN HARVEY* was a three-masted schooner commanded by Captain George Kearley of Belleoram, Newfoundland. The 143-ton craft was owned by Harvey & Company and operated out of their branch store at Belleoram, Fortune Bay.

On the night of January 9, 1912, the *John Harvey,* on a voyage from Gloucester to St. Pierre with a load of general cargo for that community, was caught in a southerly gale off the coast of Nova Scotia.

Captain Kearley and his crew had battled storms before and felt they were in no danger, for the *John Harvey* was only three years old and built to withstand winter storms. However, the storm increased to hurricane force and visibility was reduced to zero in the snow squalls. Confident that they were nowhere near land, the captain and crew were unaware that the winds and tides were bringing the ship closer and closer to the rocks, until she struck at Winning Point, Fourchu Bay, near Garabus, Nova Scotia.

The strong southerly winds drove the ship onto the rocks, where she plunged and rolled madly in the huge waves that washed over her decks. It was a wild and desolate scene that greeted the shipwrecked mariners; a boiling surf beating against the sunkers and the massive waves, tearing at the stranded ship, threatening instant destruction. Captain Kearley saw that the only chance to save their lives was to lighten the ship so that the waves would drive her closer to shore. He immediately gave the order to cut away the masts and this was done, though with some difficulty, as the rolling of the ship made it difficult to work.

The cutting away of the masts brought the ship a little closer to shore, but there still seemed to be little hope for the stranded crew. It was then that young John Foote, a Belleoram lad of seventeen, volunteered to swim ashore with a rope to try to establish a lifeline. A strong and fearless swimmer, Foote was sure he could make it to land.

With the surf beating against the rocks and the waves sweeping the deck of the doomed ship, he tied a rope around his waist and jumped into the swirling maelstrom. His anxious messmates watched as he struck out boldly for the shore, seemingly unaware of the bone chilling North Atlantic waves.

He was caught in an undertow, went under, but struggled free and, at last, a wave washed him up on the beach. Quickly, he fastened his rope to a tree and established a lifeline that his fellow crew members used to make it to shore. As soon as they had all landed safely, they looked about for some place of shelter until the storm was over. A nearby fisherman's hut offered shelter from the elements, but they had neither fire nor food to comfort them.

It was bitterly cold in the fisherman's hut and, weakened by his battle with the waves and chilled by his exposure to the bitter North Atlantic swells, John Foote and a fellow crew member, John Keeping found the effects of the numbing cold too much, and before morning, both died from the results of their exposure to the elements. Captain Kearley, his two sons and another crew member did survive the night and, next morning, walked to Gull Cove, where they told the story of the wreck of the *John Harvey* and the bravery of John Foote.

The story of the wreck of the *John Harvey* and the heroism of young John Foote was told and retold and became a part of the marine history of the Newfoundland foreign trade. Later, a song was written to commemorate the bravery of this brave young Belleoram boy.

A RESCUE BY THE SS SAGONA

The Loss of the Maggie, March 1, 1912

THE *MAGGIE* WAS A 201-TON (gross) barquentine, 114 feet long with a 22.7-foot beam and a depth of 11.7 feet, built in Troon, Scotland. The vessel was owned by James Baird Limited of St. John's and was engaged in the foreign trade.

In early December, 1912, the *Maggie* sailed from St. John's with a load of fish for Oporto. After a successful voyage across the Atlantic, she unloaded her cargo and was returning to her home port of St. John's when she ran into difficulties.

On Ash Wednesday, the crew were all busy shortening sail when one of the crew members, Patrick Mahoney, who was tying up the lee arm, lost his footing and plunged to the deck below. He was knocked unconscious by the fall and despite the captain's attempt, to revive him, died without regaining consciosness.

The body was taken to the cabin and waked until 4:00 P.M., the next day. Then the ship was hove-to and the funeral service was read by the captain. After the funeral service, Mahoney's body was consigned to the sea.

Everything went all right for a few days, but when they were about sixty-five miles from Cape Race, a terrible storm blew up. It increased from gale to hurricane force and the *Maggie* was buffeted by the high winds and heavy seas which swept over her bulwarks. In the middle of the storm the *Maggie* lost her foreyard mizzen-gaff, mainstays and practically all her rigging and canvas. Captain Connors and his men were to say later that, never in their nautical experience had they seen such a storm as that encountered by the *Maggie* on this occasion.

Eventually the storm lost most of its fury and the *Maggie,* despite the terrible battering by the elements, continued on her voyage back home to Newfoundland. The reprieve from danger was short lived, however, for two days later the vessel encountered ice and was soon jammed solid. The wind then pushed her against the ice, which cut through her port side and caused her to leak, Captain Connors ordered her cargo shifted so that she was listing towards the starboard side, with two streaks out of water. However, before repairs could be effected, the starboard side began to leak too. It was also discovered that the vessel's cutwater had been carried away and her rudder badly damaged.

Having assessed the damages to their ship, Captain Connors and his crew came to the conclusion that they were in grave danger. They were sure that as soon as the ice opened the vessel would sink. In the face of this new danger their only lifeboat was provisioned with food and water and placed on runners so she could be hauled over the ice if it became necessary to abandon ship.

Then, on Monday afternoon, the SS *Sagona* was sighted and Captain Connors sent up distress signals. There were some anxious moments on the *Maggie,* but the distress signals were seen by the *Sagona* and she began to make her way through the ice to the trapped vessel. It was a most welcome sight to captain and crew when the SS *Sagona* came alongside and they were able to leave their sinking ship.

Before leaving the *Maggie,* Captain Connors, in order to keep her from becoming a menace to navigation, set her on fire, both fore and aft. Then, the captain of the SS *Sagona* gave the burning *Maggie* a few butts which released her from the ice and she immediately sank. She had been sixty-six days out from Oporto when she went under.

It was a very grateful captain and crew who were landed in St. John's, after what had been the most harrowing voyage of their lives.

ABANDONED AT SEA

The Loss of the Schooner Tobeatic, January 22, 1914

ON OCTOBER 11, 1913, the ninety-nine-ton schooner *Tobeatic* left St. John's with a cargo of salt for Burin. After a two day run she arrived at Burin, discharged her cargo of salt and took on a load of salt fish for the European market.

The vessel under the command of Captain John White, made a quick voyage across the Atlantic, and eighteen days after leaving Burin arrived in Gibraltar. Here instructions awaited Captain White to proceed to Alicante to unload his cargo. Seven days later the *Tobeatic* reached Alicante and a week later she had discharged her cargo of fish. From there she travelled to Santa Pola and loaded a cargo of salt for St. John's.

On Christmas Day, 1913, the *Tobeatic* left for home. After a two-and-a-half-day voyage they reached Gibraltar and, after a few hours delay, left on their homeward voyage. Soon after leaving Gibraltar they ran into stormy weather, with high winds and heavy seas, but the *Tobeatic* was a sturdy ship and suffered no damage. This weather continued to buffet the schooner until January 17, 1914, when the *Tobeatic* reached the northern edge of the Gulf Stream. Here they ran into a storm so violent that it smashed her booms and gaffs and carried away all of her canvas.

Faced with this disaster, Captain White ordered a new mainsail bent, but so fierce was the storm, it lasted only a few minutes before it, too, was torn away. Once again the schooner was forced to drive before the storm. During this time a large square-rigged vessel was sighted, but her crew either didn't see or paid no attention to the distress signals flown by the *Tobeatic,* and passed on her way without offering any assistance.

The next day a steamer did come to their assistance and stayed by the *Tobeatic* for an hour, but the storm was so severe that the other ship could not be of any assistance and went on her way. Then for five terrible, gut-wrenching days the schooner was battered by the storm, and, without sails, was totally at the mercy of the elements.

On January 22, when they were about 150 miles off the Western Islands, their distress signals were seen by the oil tanker, *Leda,* which quickly came to their assistance. Captain White signalled that his ship was so badly damaged that he wanted to abandon her, and the mate of the *Leda* led a lifeboat crew to rescue the captain and crew of the ill-fated *Tobeatic.*

NINE HOURS IN A LIFEBOAT

The Loss of the Barquentine Galatea, August 19, 1915

THE BARQUENTINE *GALATEA* was owned and operated by James Baird & Company of St. John's. The vessel was engaged in the foreign trade and in the summer of 1915, she left Baird's wharf at St. John's under the command of Captain Vatcher for Santa Pola, Spain, with a load of dried fish. Although World War I was raging and enemy raiders were active, the *Galatea* escaped them and made a successful voyage to Spain. She landed her cargo without incident and then took on a load of salt for her return voyage to St. John's. She left Santa Pola on August 14, 1915, and once more, successfully escaped the attention of enemy raiders and submarines.

The first few days of the return voyage they had favourable winds, but then the weather changed. It became very stormy and the *Galatea* was battered by wind and waves. As the voyage proceeded the storm increased in violence and the ship could carry very little canvas. Under these conditions, the ship became difficult to manage. By August 19, when she was only five days out of port the constant strain on the ship began to tell and she started to leak.

Immediately the crew manned the pumps and the ship's officers attempted to assess the extent of the damage the ship had suffered. They couldn't find the damaged area, but it was soon evident that the water was coming in faster than the men could pump it out and it became clear that the *Galatea* would soon sink. Under these circumstances Captain Vatcher had no option but to order his men to prepare a lifeboat in readiness to abandon the ship.

A number of the crew quickly provisioned the lifeboat and got her ready to launch. While they were doing this, the rest of the crew kept the pumps going.

When everything was ready, Captain Vatcher gave the order to abandon ship. The lifeboat was launched and the captain and crew took their places. It was only six hours since the leaks had been discovered, but the *Galatea* was about to go under.

Captain Vatcher and crew rowed away from the sinking ship and not too long after they had left her, she plunged to the bottom. The captain noted they were now in Latitude 36 degrees 37 minutes west and Longitude 3 minutes 3 degrees north, with not a ship in sight to come to their aid.

For nine hours Captain Sandy Vatcher and his crew consisting of George Matthews, John Buckland, Earnest Simel, John Lamb and Albert Noseworthy, huddled in the lifeboat taking turns at the oars and hoping a ship soon would appear on the horizon. It was a long wait, and they were becoming a little despondent, when, at last a ship came into view. They quickly sent up distress signals and the ship saw them and came to their aid.

The rescue ship was the *Dunster,* bound for Cardiff, Wales. She took the shipwrecked crew on board and landed them at Cardiff, where they were very well treated. From Cardiff, the men contacted the firm of James Baird & Sons and reported the loss of their ship and their rescue by the *Dunster.*

The authorities at Cardiff treated the shipwrecked sailors very well and arranged for the men to travel to Liverpool to take passage on the SS *Carthaginian* for St. John's. They arrived safely, none the worse for their nine hour ordeal in a lifeboat in the North Atlantic.

CHRISTMAS DAY IN A LIFEBOAT

The Loss of the E.S. Hocken, December 14, 1917

CAPTAIN SAMUEL COURTNEY was one of Newfoundland's most successful and experienced master mariners when he took command of the *E.S. Hocken*. She was a brigantine of some 250 tons, and Captain Courtney was part owner, holding fifteen shares, while A.S. Rendell & Company acted as managing owners. The *E.S. Hocken* was a fine old vessel that, in 1914, had been repaired and reclassed. Captain Courtney thought her to be a first class ship, but he was soon to find otherwise.

On January 10, 1917, the *Hocken* loaded 5,500 drums of dried fish and set sail for Bahia, Brazil. They had not been at sea very long when Captain Courtney was surprised and taken aback to find that, as soon as the vessel got her speed up to more than six knots no one on the ship could steer her. This resulted in a slow passage to Brazil, which she reached after a voyage of forty-two days.

After the usual delays, they finished discharging their cargo of fish, loaded ballast and sailed to Barbados, where they took on a cargo of 700 puncheons of molasses for St. John's. They left Barbados on April 7, and the return voyage was worse than the voyage down to Brazil. In fact, the voyage home was a veritable nightmare. The ship was rolling badly all the time and some of the tiers of cargo shifted, which caused a heavy starboard list. They had to jettison some of the puncheons of molasses to try and get her as far as possible on an even keel. It was dangerous work, as the puncheons were constantly on the move. However, they did make it back to St. John's and unloaded the cargo of molasses.

In July, the *Hocken* again sailed for Brazil and arrived at Pernambuco after a voyage of forty-eight days. They unloaded their cargo and then Captain Courtney accepted a charter to load a cargo of tobacco at Bahia, for Cadiz, Spain. As it was wartime and enemy raiders and submarines were active, they loaded for a lump sum freight, payable in advance. When the ship was loaded they set sail for Spain.

Everything went well until they were between Madeira and the Azores Islands. Here, a sudden squall from what seemed to the Newfoundland crew a clear sky, tore away most of their sails. It took the crew until the next day to rig new sails. Then, to their horror they smelled smoke and, on investigating discovered that the cargo of tobacco was on fire.

Captain Courtney immediately took what measures he could to keep the fire contained. He ordered the hatches taken off the holds and, in an attempt to contain the fire, filled the decks with tobacco and threw some of it overboard. However, it was soon discovered that the fire had eaten too deep into the cargo to be put out. Under the circumstances, the only thing to do was to re-stow the tobacco they had taken out on deck, close the hatches and make for the nearest port.

It was an anxious time for Captain Vatcher and his crew, but they made it to Cadiz. Immediately, there was a new problem. The Spanish authorities refused to let them go alongside a wharf for some days, fearing the Hocken would burst into flames. Finally, Captain Courtney was able to convince the port authorities there was no danger from the fire, and they were allowed to unload their cargo, which consisted of what H.F. Shortis, in his account of the voyage, called "Tobacco already smoked!"

The ship suffered no damage from the burning tobacco, and they loaded a cargo of salt for Newfoundland. Because of the danger from German raiders, the Spanish Port Authorities allowed them to sail after dark, and gave them a route to follow to avoid the German submarines in the area. They carefully followed the route given them and saw no submarines or any other ships. Feeling they were now safe, Captain Courtney shaped his course for St. John's. There was only one ill omen of what was to come, and that was that the rats which had been on the *Hocken* had all deserted her in Cadiz.

However, everything went well for the first two weeks of the return voyage. They had a fair wind and were making good progress, when, like a bolt from the blue, disaster struck. It was a Sunday morning and all hands had gathered round to take a turn at the pumps. This was a routine activity but, on this occasion they "got a suck," as the sailors put it. They waited half an hour and then started in again. This time there could be no doubt, the ship was leaking. The sailors listened carefully and said they could hear water running in.

The captain ordered some of the cargo of salt brought on deck, which gave the ship sufficient list so they could examine her down near to her keelson. They cut out the ceiling, but could not find the leak. Then they searched for an open butt or seam, but again, with no success. However, the ship was leaking badly and it soon became apparent they might have to throw the cargo of salt overboard and try to make it to Barbados, which was the nearest port.

However, after a few hours with the water rising rapidly in the hold, the captain decided that there was no point in jettisoning the cargo, for the ship was doomed. He ordered two lifeboats prepared for launching. One was an eighteen-foot boat, the other fourteen feet. Captain Courtney also suggested that the crew line the sides of the boat with canvas to give them some shelter. The boats were also provisioned for a long voyage, as they were about 900 miles away from Barbados.

Anxiously, the crew waited for the order to abandon ship. On Saturday, December 12, just one week after they had discovered the leak, they sounded the pump, and found six feet of water in the hold. On Monday, December 14, Captain Courtney gave the order to abandon ship. The two lifeboats were swung out and Captain Courtney and his crew manned them. Before leaving the *Hocken,* it was decided to set fire to her to prevent her becoming a menace to navigation. This was done and the two boats rowed away from the burning vessel. There were five men in the larger boat and three in the smaller one.

They rigged a sail on each boat and set their course for Barbados, 900 miles away. They encountered some strong headwinds, and once, when it rained heavily, the cook filled his rubber boots with water in order to help stretch their water supply.

Christmas Day found them many miles from land, with only a ration of mouldy bread and water for their Christmas dinner. Sadly, the men thought of how their families would be enjoying Christmas Day at home with plenty of good food and drink, and they especially missed the "sweet bread," the special Christmas treat of all Newfoundlanders.

However, undaunted by the grim conditions, they kept their way and, on December 29, 1917 they arrived at Barbados. They had spent fifteen days in the lifeboats. The men presented a forlorn appearance when they came into the Bay of Carsiole. Here they had to wait an hour before they could land, as the government doctor was having a bath on the beach and would not come to attend to them until he was finished. Taking pity on their condition, the captain of one ship in the harbour invited them aboard his ship for a bite to eat, but the Harbour Police would not permit it until the shipwrecked crew had a clearance from the doctor.

Finally, the doctor came and they were allowed to land. They spent a week on the island and then took passage on the SS *Chaleur* which was bound to Saint John, New Brunswick. From Saint John they were returned to their homes in Newfoundland. Following this harrowing experience, Captain Courtney, though still in the prime of life, retired from the sea and took up farming in Kilbride.

RESCUED JUST IN TIME

The Loss of the Motor Schooner Bianca, October 31, 1919

ON OCTOBER 21, 1919, the motor schooner, *Bianca,* under the command of Captain Mark Burke, with a crew of eight men. sailed from Indian Harbour, Labrador. The 408-ton auxiliary schooner carried a cargo of 10,500 quintals of dried fish, and was bound for the port of Gibraltar, where Captain Burke was to receive further orders on where to deliver his cargo.

During the first two days of the voyage the vessel experienced good weather. The wind was westerly and under full sail with her motor running, the *Bianca* was making good time. However things soon changed. On Thursday, October 23, the winds backed to the east and the ship experienced heavy swells coming in from the south. At 4:00 P.M. the captain had the crew try the pumps to make sure they were not taking on water. The pumps came up dry. Then it became necessary to tack, but under full sail, with the engine going, the vessel was dipping her bows and taking some water on deck.

At 6:00 P.M. the engineer reported that there was water over the ship's keelson. They immediately sounded the area and found three feet of water in the ship's hold. Captain Burke stopped the engine and all hands manned the bilge pump, the hand pump, and the forward engine pump. Two hours later the pumps sucked dry. Then, an hour later, the engine running the bilge pump stopped and could not be repaired. With the bilge pump out of commission the hand pumps and forward engine pump could not keep up with the rising water in the hold.

Around 5:00 A.M on Friday, October 24, the water was gaining so rapidly, the captain ordered the jettisoning of some cargo to lighten the ship. All day Friday the weather was fine, with a moderate south wind, but the water continued to rise in the hold. At 5:00 P.M. Friday, Captain Burke decided to run for the nearest land. The ship's position was now 51.30 degrees north, latitude and longitude was 49.39 degrees west. Captain Burke set the course northwest, and with full sails and the engine running, they hoped to be able to make land.

However, around midnight the wind changed and a strong gale blew up from the north. At 4:00 A.M. on Saturday, the storm which was now from the northeast, forced them to change their course to southwest. Captain Burke ordered the crew to cut through the bulkhead to jettison more cargo. With 1,200 quintals of fish thrown overboard, the ship became more buoyant and did not labour so heavily in the seas.

It was now decided that, with the ship handling better, they would try and make Gibraltar. So on Monday, October 27, with a westerly wind, all sails set, the engine running and the crew manning the pumps, Captain Burke set his course for Gibraltar. That night the wind died down and the ocean became dead calm.

At 8:00 A.M. on Tuesday they lowered the sails but kept the engine going. The seas remained calm until Wednesday, when a storm blew up from the southwest. The sails were hoisted and the captain set a close reefed mainsail and storm sail and hove the vessel to, to ride out the gale. At noon the wind veered to the west and once again the *Bianca* was labouring in heavy seas. The pumps were constantly going, and after midnight the gale increased. About 8:00 A.M. Thursday a mountainous sea struck the ship, breaking the mainboom and tearing the mainsail to shreds. The same sea smashed the lifeboats to splinters and tore away the poop rail. It broke the cabin skylight and also swept away the engine room companionway, flooded the engine room and stopped the bilge pump engine as well as the main engine.

To make matters worse, the force of the wave tore open the ship's sides and the ship's company now had to rely on their hand pumps to keep the ship afloat. A tremendous sea ran all night, but the crew kept the pumps going and did wonders under such difficult circumstances.

At 4:00 A.M on October 31, the wind began to increase and at 8:00 P.M. they hoisted the fore staysail and lower mizzen storm sail and set a course for the southeast. The wind kept up and the ship ran under a foresail until about 6:00 P.M., when the lights of a steamer were sighted. Around 7:00 P.M. the steamer was about a mile from the *Bianca* and Captain Burke sent up a distress flare. To their great delight the steamer changed course and came towards them. It was the SS *Lehigh*.

On reaching the *Bianca* and learning that her lifeboats had been smashed, a crew of men from the SS *Lehigh* volunteered to take them off the sinking ship. They launched one of the steamer's lifeboats and were successful in taking off the captain and crew of the *Bianca*. Captain James Deal, of the *Lehigh,* welcomed the crew of the *Bianca* and made them as comfortable as possible. The ship was bound for Charleston, South Carolina.

The shipwrecked crew were taken to the crew's quarters of the *Lehigh,* given dry underwear and put in the crew's bunks to rest and regain their strength. They arrived at Charleston, and later returned to Newfoundland.

In an interview with the *Evening Telegram* Captain Burke and his crew offered their wholehearted thanks to Captain James Deal and his crew for their humane and kind treatment. Captain Burke summed it all up by saying, "The traditions of the sea were nobly maintained by the master of the *Lehigh* and his gallant crew."

A NIGHT OF TERROR

The Sparkling Glance Abandoned, February 9, 1921

IN FEBRUARY OF 1921, CAPTAIN REG KEEPING of Belleoram and his crew had a narrow escape from death, when their schooner, the *Sparkling Glance,* became disabled in mid-Atlantic and threatened to plunge to the bottom during a winter storm.

Although still a young man, Captain Reg. Keeping was an experienced foreign-going captain who had had his schooner, *Thomas,* sunk in the Mediterranean by a German U-boat during World War I. His crew members were Harold Baker, James Buffett, William Cluett, S. Poole, Stanley Bond and Henry Carter, the cook, all from Belleoram, Fortune Bay.

The *Sparkling Glance* was a three-masted schooner built in 1918 for Harvey & Company of St. John's. Harvey's operated a branch establishment at Belleoram and many a cargo of fish was exported to the foreign markets from that port.

In mid-January, the *Sparkling Glance* loaded 4,000 quintals of dried fish for Oporto and set sail from Belleoram. She had a good crossing until the evening of February 5, when she ran into a vicious winter storm, which continued all night. The winds reached hurricane force and it took all of Captain Keeping's skill and the hard work of his crew to keep the vessel head on to the storm. It was hoped that when dawn broke on February 6, the winds would abate a little. Instead, they increased, and Henry Carter, the cook, later said that neither Captain Keeping nor his crew had ever experienced such a raging blizzard as they did on that morning.

Shortly after daylight, the high winds carried away the bowsprit rigging, and shortly after that a huge waves smashed her rudder, leaving the schooner unmanageable in a raging hurricane. Captain Keeping and his crew were powerless to make any repairs during the storm, and felt every moment might be their last.

The huge waves crashed down on their rudderless vessel, causing her to tremble from stem to stern with the force of the impact. When this happened the crippled *Sparkling Glance* would wallow in the trough of the surging waves only to be lifted high on the succeeding foam-capped wave before again disappearing in the trough of the waves that followed. In this situation, the captain and crew could only cling to the rigging and pray for deliverance.

Under such circumstances, eating was out of the question, as the ship's forecastle was badly flooded. For twenty-four hours the hungry crew fought to keep from being washed overboard. Then, slowly the storm began to abate, and a prayer of thanksgiving went up from the half-frozen, drenched men. They bailed out their forecastle and the cook was able to prepare a meal for his starving shipmates.

The fair weather continued into February 8 and immediately Captain Keeping, with the help of his crew, improvised a method of steering the vessel. Everything was beginning to get back to normal when, on the evening of February 8, another storm came up. At this unwanted turn of events, dismay again struck the captain and crew of the battered *Sparkling Spray*. They knew that there was no way their improvised steering mechanism could survive a storm. By dusk, the *Sparkling Spray* was again totally at the mercy of the wind and waves and it seemed that she might not last out the night.

In this desperate situation distress flares were sent up, but neither captain nor crew expected that help would come in time. Then, from about a mile away, an answering flare appeared, signalling that help was near, if they could weather this latest storm. All through that desperate night, with each man on the doomed vessel fearing each moment might be his last, the flares from the nearby ship gave them a ray of hope and comfort.

Finally, dawn broke on the morning of February 9, and the crew of the American steamer SS *Liberty Lord* prepared to come to their rescue. The seas were still running mountainously high, but a lifeboat was launched from the American ship. It took an hour of battling the heavy seas before the lifeboat made it to the side of the *Sparkling Glance* and took her captain and crew on board. It was an equally difficult passage back to the steamer, but eventually, all hands were safe on board.

The captain and crew of the *Liberty Lord* welcomed the crew of the *Sparkling Glance* and did everything they could to help them after their harrowing ordeal. They were taken to Bermuda, and from there, given passage back to St. John's. As both Captain Keeping and his crew were from Belleoram, they took passage back home on the SS *Kyle.*

THE VOYAGES AND WRECK OF THE GENERAL CURRIE, 1918-1922

IN THE WINTER OF 1918, the 195-ton tern schooner, *General Currie* was built at Grand Bank for the firm of Samuel Harris Ltd. of that town. The master builder was Eli Harris, a brother to Samuel Harris, the owner, and the ship was intended for the foreign fish trade. On completion, the ship was placed under the command of Captain Clarence Williams and he continued to command the vessel for the next four years.

On one of her first return voyages from Portugal in 1919, Captain Williams rescued the five-man crew of the schooner *Burleigh* which had become a water soaked hulk and sank shortly after her crew had been rescued.

The *General Currie* continued under the command of Captain Clarence Williams and made a number of successful Atlantic voyages. However times were changing in the Newfoundland export fishery, and government inspectors now decided the quality of the fish that could be exported and set the asking price. On a voyage in the fall of 1920, the *General Currie* loaded 5,074 quintals of salt fish at Lamaline for the Lisbon market. On that voyage the firm of Samuel Harris lost over $42,000,00. Markets for the exported salt fish continued poor. Salt fish glutted the traditional European markets lowering the price and sometimes making it difficult to find a buyer at any price.

In the autumn of 1921,the *General Currie* set sail for Portugal with a cargo of dry fish. Two of the crew members were Frank Hynes and his brother Leo, both natives of Bay L'Argent, Fortune Bay. Frank was a young war veteran who had been wounded and captured at the Battle of Monchy, in April 1917. After the war he returned home to Bay L'Argent and went to sea.

Under the command of Captain Clarence Williams, the *General Currie* had an uneventful voyage across the Atlantic and anchored at the mouth of the Tagus River. They did not tie up at the dock because it would make it easier for thieves to attack the ship and rob the crew.

On their arrival, they found that a national strike had been called and it lasted for seventy-four days. This meant that nothing could be done until the strike ended. One day Frank and his brother, Leo saw a body floating in the Tagus river. They secured the body and then reported their find to the Lisbon authorities. They were immediately questioned very closely, and even accused of murder. It took a lot of talking to persuade the police that they were innocent.

When the two suspects were finally cleared, Captain Williams warned his crew that if, in future, they saw a dead body in the river they were to leave it alone.

Finally the strike was over. They landed their cargo of fish and then set sail for home. Captain Williams decided to set his course from the Canary Islands. There are two tides flowing around the islands, one east and one west. Captain Williams followed the west tide and this took them to the Sargasso Sea, where they were becalmed for two weeks.

During this period, Captain Williams kept the crew busy painting the vessel and cleaning up her decks. Finally, their luck changed and a brisk breeze sprang up. Captain Williams set his course for Fortune Bay and arrived safely at Grand Bank. There was great rejoicing on their arrival home, for they had been given up as lost.

Shortly after this voyage, Frank and Leo Hynes emigrated to the United States. They continued to go to sea and, in a few years became foreign-going captains, who could take a ship to any part of the world.

On March 30, 1922, the *General Currie* was on a another voyage to Europe, still under the command of Captain Clarence Williams. A storm blew up shortly after they left port and the *General Currie* drove ashore on Dog Island, near St. Pierre. The schooner was a total loss, but Captain Williams and his crew all managed to get on shore safely.

ALMOST HOME

The Loss of the Schooner Asquith, Winter 1922

IN 1920, THE FINEST SHIP IN THE FLEET of twenty-one vessels owned by the firm of A.E. Hickman was the 271-ton tern schooner, *Asquith*.

The *Asquith* was built in Bridgewater, Nova Scotia in 1916, and shortly after her launching became part of the Hickman fleet. The tern schooner was painted white and could carry a load of 8,000 quintals of dried fish.

In the fall of 1920, the *Asquith*, under the command of Captain Arthur Snelgrove, returned from a foreign voyage and was sent to Nova Scotia for a load of coal. The Sydney trip would take about a month, and when the *Asquith* arrived back in St. John's, there would likely be another load of fish ready for Europe or Brazil.

The ship sailed from St. John's, and then it seemed as if she had disappeared off the face of the ocean. Days grew into weeks, weeks into months, and Captain Arthur Snelgrove and his crew were given up for lost. Then came a telegram from Barbados, saying that the *Asquith* had put in there for repairs. The telegram sparked a lot of wonderment; what was Captain Snelgrove doing in Barbados, 2,000 miles from his intended destination? The answer was that the ship had encountered a series of severe storms and it was only through the skill of the captain and his crew that they had weathered them all, and finally made port in Barbados.

In fact, the voyage was not a total loss for A.E. Hickman, for the *Asquith* loaded a cargo of molasses for Nova Scotia and then took on a load of coal for St. John's. The cargo of coal that should have been delivered for Christmas of the year before was finally landed in St. John's the following spring.

This was Captain Snelgrove's last voyage in the *Asquith*. He was promoted to manage Hickman's West End Premises in St. John's. This job meant that he had to oversee the vessels in the Hickman fleet. In his new position, he sometimes had to reprimand the skippers of the other schooners. On one occasion he was pointing out to another skipper that he wasn't doing his job as he should. The other skipper shot back, "But I always got where they sent me," a sharp reminder of the Barbados incident.

The skipper who succeeded Captain Snelgrove as master of the *Asquith* was Captain Isaac Thornhill of Grand Bank. He liked his new assignment and found the *Asquith* a good ship. In the fall of 1921, the *Asquith* went to Quirpon to take on a cargo of what was called, "Labrador slop" for the Spanish market.

The voyage across the Atlantic was uneventful and the ship behaved beautifully. After unloading the fish, Captain Thornhill took on a load of 500 tons of salt and sailed for home.

The return voyage was uneventful until the ship was nearly home. Then disaster struck. The winter gales of 1922 were terrible, but the *Asquith,* a sturdy, well-built ship, weathered them all until almost home.

Then a sudden storm swept the ocean, and Captain Thornhill was forced to heave to under double reefs to ride out the gale. The storm was so fierce the captain was afraid that the vessel's trysail would be carried away. He set his men to work preparing a new one, just in case the worst happened. Then, the captain's worst fears were realized. A monstrous wave came up and pitched in the mainsail. It tore the sail to ribbons, smashed off the booms and filled the deck with water. One of the crew, a West Indian seaman, was washed overboard and drowned. Captain Thornhill was swept through the smashed cabin door into a water-filled cabin. He was able to keep his head above water and held on until the water receded. It later took hours to bail out the cabin and make it liveable again.

While the storm raged they could do nothing but try to ride it out. However, when it abated they tried the pumps and found that it took much longer to pump out the schooner than before. It was clear that the ship was strained and was now leaking badly. As the day wore on it took longer and longer to pump and they could no longer free the vessel. It became apparent that their ship would sink.

There was only one hope of survival, so Captain Thornhill put the schooner before the wind and headed for the track followed by the steamers. For four days they pumped for their lives and strained to see if there was any sign of a passing steamer. On the fourth night after the storm, the men saw the lights of a vessel, but she was passing them. They could tell that the unknown ship was travelling parallel to them.

The bosun then took a flare and went aloft with it. The flare was seen and, to the joy of the men on the sinking *Asquith,* the ship changed course and came towards them. When she came alongside, it proved to be the SS *Arcturus,* an American cargo ship bound for India via the Suez Canal. They launched a lifeboat and soon had Captain Thornhill and his men on board the steamer. The rescue came none too soon, for in a short while the *Asquith* slipped beneath the waves.

When the *Arcturus* was off Gibraltar, the captain signalled for a boat to come out. The boat took the shipwrecked sailors back to Gibraltar and there, arrangements were made for their return passage and they travelled home by the SS *Digby*. They arrived back in St. John's on St. Patrick's Day, in the middle of a severe snowstorm.

Captain Thornhill continued to go to sea and, during World War II, he was in command of the *Emily,* which was sailing in convoy to England. The convoy was attacked by enemy U-boats, but Captain Thornhill evaded the enemy and delivered the *Emily* to the Royal Navy.

A CLOSE SHAVE

The Loss of the Schooner Kinsman, December 4, 1922

THE *KINSMAN* WAS A three-masted schooner owned by A.E Hickman & Company and engaged in the foreign trade. On November 19, 1922 she left Battle Harbour, Labrador, for Gibraltar with 8,000 quintals of dried fish in her hold. The ship's company was made up of Captain M. Picco, master, Noah Blake, mate, Alf Payne, bosun, J. Yarn, cook and seamen Joseph Picco, Jack Mullins and Philip Cheeseman.

The voyage to Gibraltar was uneventful until November 25, when a heavy northwest gale sprang up with heavy seas. For two days and nights the storm raged, and the *Kinsman* was badly buffeted by the elements. Huge waves swept over her deck with such force that her seams opened and she began to leak. The crew had to man the pumps in shifts in order to keep the ship dry. In fact, even with the pumps going day and night the water continued to rise steadily in her hold.

Faced with this situation, Captain Picco debated with himself whether they should try to make Gibraltar or head for the nearest land. After consulting with the mate and crew it was decided that the best course of action was to keep pumping, crowd on all possible sails and run for the Azores which offered the nearest port. If the weather and their luck held they should be able to make it.

The crew worked the pumps for all they were worth, but still the water rose steadily in the hold. Then, on December 1, 1922, the SS *Guild Rosa* from Jamaica bound to le Harve, France, was sighted. Captain Picco signalled the steamer for a correct position. The schooner hove to and mate Blake rowed over to the steamer to interview the ship's officers regarding their position.

While the mate was talking to the captain and officers of the *Guild Rosa* the schooner and the steamer came too close together and because of poor management on the part of the steamer's crew, the *Guild Rosa* collided with the *Kinsman* and tore away her bowsprit and did other minor damages. When the wreckage was cleared away the captain of the *Guild Rosa* advised Captain Picco to abandon his vessel and go on board the steamer.

However, Captain Picco and his crew were determined, as long as there was any possibility of the ship staying afloat, to try to make land. When the captain of the *Guild Rosa* saw that his offer of assistance was not acceptable to Captain Picco, he steamed away, after promising to report their position by wireless, which he did.

The *Kinsman* was now about 350 miles from the Azores and it looked as if Captain Picco and his crew would make it. With all sails set and the pump crews working in relays they felt sure they would make their destination. Then, on the evening of December 2, another southwest gale sprang up and began buffeting the *Kinsman*.

As the storm increased in violence the crashing waves began to force apart the planking on the *vessel* and she began to leak very badly. In fact, when they took a sounding it was discovered that she now had four and a half feet of water in her hold.

The men redoubled their efforts at the pumps, but the water in the hold kept gaining and Captain Picco knew they were in serious trouble. As the water mounted in the hold the ship began to slowly sink by the head. However, there was still some hope of making land, for at noon on December 3, they sighted Santa Maria about thirty-five miles distant. But the water kept gaining and it was soon apparent that the ship would not make land. The captain and crew still undaunted, kept the ship moving and getting closer and closer to safety. All that long dark night they kept the ship moving, but because the wind was unfavourable and the bows of the *Kinsman* were now nearly underwater they made little progress towards land.

At 5:00 A.M. on December 4 with the *Kinsman* still a good distance from land and threatening every minute to dip her bows beneath the waves, the Portuguese steamship *Gilannes* came in sight.

By now it was only a matter of minutes before the vessel sank and Captain Picco and his crew gladly took refuge on the *Gilannes*. Only a few minutes later the *Kinsman* disappeared beneath the waves.

The shipwrecked crew received excellent treatment from the captain and crew of their rescue ship. They were taken to Madeira and afterwards travelled to Lisbon. At Lisbon they joined a steamer for Liverpool and were then given passage on the SS *Minnedoda* to Saint John, New Brunswick. From here they took passage by train for St. John's.

Fate, however was not finished with them, and on their way across Newfoundland they were involved in a train wreck. Captain Picco suffered a gash to his head that required four stitches. A fellow passenger on the train was Sir. P.T. McGrath, who did everything he could to make the shipwrecked crew comfortable.

They arrived by the *Overland Express* at St. John's on January 3, 1923. It was a voyage that neither Captain Picco nor his crew would ever forget.

A STRANGE TALE OF THE SEA

The Sinking of the Workman, January 1922

THE *WORKMAN* WAS A three-masted schooner built by the Chauk shipyard at Charlottetown, Bonavista Bay. She was considered to be one of the most beautiful schooners ever built there. J.T. Swyers of Bonavista financed the shipyard and usually kept some shares in the vessels built there, but A.E. Hickman Company was the managing owners and the ship flew the Hickman flag.

The vessel was launched in September of 1920 and Captain George Anstey of Grand Bank took command of her. The *Workman* was soon engaged in the foreign trade, taking cargoes of fish to European ports.

In early January 1922, The *Workman* loaded 3,500 quintals of dried fish for the Spanish market and, under the command of Captain Anstey, set out for the port of Seville in Spain. They encountered good weather all across the Atlantic and were only about a day's sail from the Straits of Gibraltar when disaster struck.

It was a clear January evening with a good breeze blowing and, under full sail, the *Workman* was ploughing through the waves. As it was the "Dog Watch" all hands were on deck except for the cook, who was in the galley. Captain Anstey was standing near his brother, Charlie, who was mate, watching the approaching lights of a large steamer. He didn't feel his vessel was in any danger for the right of way of a sailing schooner over a steamer is a well-established principle in international waters. However, as the lights kept coming closer and there was no indication that she was going to change course, Captain Anstey sounded an alarm. "Charlie," he said to his brother, "quick, get a flare up." In a matter of minutes an oil fire was burning above the rail of the *Workman* which could be seen twenty kilometres away. The boatswain also made a flare, but the steamer kept coming toward them. The men also blew the fog horn, but it made no difference, the steamer kept on course and was going to cut them down.

Captain George Anstey was a quick thinking man. He saw that the steamer had a "flush deck," that its rails ran all around her sides, and he knew their only hope was to catch those rails and board the colliding vessel.

"Quick boys, all hands in the rigging and jump when she goes by," he ordered and remembering, that the cook was in the galley, he called him on deck with the same order. Captain Anstey and his crew went up the rigging just as the steamer, loaded with 10,000 tons of coal, struck the *Workman,* cut through her side and halfway through her cabin house. The impact swung the schooner around so that they were broadside to the steamer and Captain Anstey gave the order to jump. All hands grabbed the rails of the steamer and swung themselves onto her deck. When Captain Anstey went to the bridge there was no one there but the helmsman. Captain Anstey asked him if he knew he had run down a schooner? He said "yes," he knew they were going to collide, but there was no officer to tell him to change course.

Captain Anstey then went below and, in a small room of the galley found the mate, who was supposed to be on the bridge, drinking beer with the engineer and a few other officers. They were not even aware the steamer had cut down a schooner. He went to the captain's room and when the captain saw him he asked, "Where did you come from?" and Captain Anstey answered, "From the three-masted schooner your ship just cut down."

The captain just shook his head, saying, "It can't be, it can't be."

The steamer proved to be the SS *Maryland* and she took Captain Anstey and his crew on to Madeira. From there they took passage to Lisbon and then on to Liverpool, England. The mate who had neglected his duty also went to England.

A court case to decide who was at fault and had to pay damages was heard in the Admiralty Court. Captain Anstey spent twenty-nine days in Liverpool, defending himself against charges that he was at fault. As he later told his friend, Captain Tom Goodyear, of the twenty-nine days in Liverpool he kissed the Bible for twenty-eight of them, meaning he spent most of the time in court.

One of the pieces of evidence produced in court was the running lights of the *Workman*. They had been knocked free on impact and had fallen to the deck of the SS *Maryland*. They were now produced in court and the lawyers for the *Maryland*'s owners argued they had measured the wicks in the running lamps and they measured three-quarters of an inch instead of the full one inch wick demanded by the Board of Trade. This was a damning piece of evidence.

However, Captain Anstey was able to refute this testimony by showing that the running lights had been manufactured by an English firm that operated only about three blocks from the courthouse. They testified that the wicks were, indeed, of regulation size, and it was normal that, after filling with oil they be reduced to three quarters of an inch. It was also demonstrated that the running lights could be seen a long way away and gave ample warning to an oncoming ship to change course.

Captain Anstey won the case and his men received compensation for their lost wages, as did A E. Hickman Company for their lost ship and cargo.

Captain Anstey returned to Newfoundland and was soon in command of another ship. However, when an opening came in the St. John's Harbour Pilotage Service, Captain Anstey came ashore and, for thirty years, piloted ships in and out of the St. John's Narrows. It was Captain Anstey who brought in the *Edmund B. Alexander* when she arrived with the first contingent of American serviceman in January, 1941. Up to that time, the *Edmund B. Alexander* was the biggest ship to enter the Narrows. It required great skill and timing to get her safely into St. John's Harbour, and the American Government awarded Captain Anstey a citation for his navigational skills.

THE LAST VOYAGE OF THE A.B. BARTEAU,
February 20, 1923

ON MONDAY, FEBRUARY 5, 1923, the schooner, *A.B. Barteau*, left Perth Amboy, New York, under the command of Captain Thomas Janes. The schooner carried a load of coal for St. John's.

The vessel had a clear run for the first four days of her voyage, but on February 9 she encountered ice off the Newfoundland coast and became trapped in it. For a week, the schooner was helpless in the grip of the ice floes. Then the wind changed and the schooner again made it to open water. Everything was going well and she was making such good time that, on the morning of

February 20, Captain Janes remarked they should be in St. John's by the following day. Then, without warning disaster struck when the ship hit an ice pan which stove in her port bow.

As soon as the ship struck the ice pan, Captain Janes rushed forward and crawled out on the bowsprit to estimate the extent of the damage his ship had suffered in the collision. One look was enough to tell him the vessel was doomed, and he gave the order to abandon ship. They immediately set about launching the lifeboat, but, so swiftly did the schooner fill with water, the deck was awash before the lifeboat was fully launched. This forced the captain and crew to jump on the slob ice surrounding their vessel. The captain had a narrow escape from drowning when he jumped from the sinking schooner and went to his waist through the slob ice. The rest of the crew had their boots filled with water. They had just made it to the ice when the *A.B. Barteau* disappeared beneath the waves, leaving them stranded about 100 miles from land.

The lifeboat had floated free shortly before the ship went down and the men were able to haul her up on the ice. Dragging the boat in case they came upon ice lakes or open water between the ice pans, they set out to find land.

Captain Janes and his men walked until night fall, when sheer exhaustion forced them to stop and rest. They built a shelter with small pieces of ice, spread out an oil-coat and then huddled close together for warmth. It was a bitterly cold night and, with their wet clothes and feet frozen in their wet boots they got little sleep.

The next morning they decided it was best to abandoned the lifeboat, as dragging her along was slowing them down. However, before leaving the boat they took the oars and left the following message attached to her:

> *A.B. Barteau* foundered Feb. 20th. Crew left ship on the ice and are walking in the hope of reaching land. Finder of this boat please communicate with the British Consul or A.B. Rendell of St. John's.

Having left this message, they started out again and bravely, continued on in the hope of finding land. When night fell they stopped again, built another ice shelter and once again tried to rest. The next morning some of the men had become frozen in the ice and had to be cut free.

As darkness fell on their third night on the ice, the men again built a crude ice shelter. It was another bitterly cold night and weak, from hunger, they felt that, unless help came quickly they were doomed. However, the mate, Leonard Dale, encouraged the men, saying he had a premonition that help was near, and he would stay on watch all night.

Around 3:00 A.M. his faith was rewarded, when he saw a ship's light some distance away. He immediately roused his companions and they set about preparing a distress signal. The only thing they had to burn was the oil coat that had served as a ground sheet. They wrapped the oil coat around an oar, ignited it and prayed it would be seen from the passing ship. Anxiously, they waited, and then a great cheer went up as the lights of the ship came towards them.

The ship they had sighted was the Norwegian steamer, SS *Hauk* under the command of Captain Alsten. She had left Louisbourg on February 17 for St. John's, but, after rounding the western end of Sable Island, ran into ice which slowed her progress. On Thursday, February 22, she was about 120 miles west south west of Cape Pine. Here they encountered bays of water alternating with ice and the captain changed his course to east north east. By nightfall the *Hauk* was about eighty miles off Cape Pine. Here they ran into tightly packed ice and the *Hauk* made little progress.

It was the mate of the *Hauk* who first saw the burning oil jacket and he called Captain Alsten, who was below at the time. The captain came on deck and quickly realized that a distress signal was being burned. Immediately, he changed course and tried to push his ship through the ice in the direction of the distress signal.

However, after two hours of steam he had to give way and wait for daybreak. As daylight broke they could make out a number of men standing huddled together on a pan of ice behind an ice shelter. Occasionally, one of the men would fall, and be picked up by his companions. Seeing this, the captain of the *Hauk* knew the men must be in a desperate plight and, throwing caution to the winds, forced his ship through the ice to the pan on which the men had taken shelter, and they were quickly helped aboard the *Hauk*.

The men were suffering badly from frostbite and weak with hunger. The captain and crew of the *Hauk* did everything they could to make the castaways comfortable. They cut away their frozen clothing and boots and then gave them hot brandy. Then they fed them slowly with hot gruel. The crew of the *Hauk* then rubbed the men's frozen feet with snow, and some were so badly frostbitten it was eight hours before all the frost had been drawn from their limbs. When this task was finished, Captain Janes and his crew were placed in the bunks which the crew of the *Hauk* had given up to them.

The frostbitten men were in desperate need of medical attention, but the weather turned stormy. On Saturday, February 24, with the wind from the west north west, the ice became tightly packed, and on Sunday, February 25, the *Hauk* became jammed tight in the ice. For six days she remained trapped, unable to move. All this time the agonies of the suffering castaways from the *A.B. Barteau* can only be imagined. Finally, on March 30, the ice loosened and the *Hauk* was in clear water near Cape Race. It took another two days to punch her way to St. John's.

On arrival, the captain and crew of the *A.B. Barteau* were treated on board the *Hauk* by Doctors Carnell and Knight. Captain Janes, the cook, John Hynes and seaman John Vatcher were in bad shape and had to be sent to the General Hospital for further treatment. Seaman Parrot, who was not as serious as the other three was sent to the Sudbury hospital. Leonard Daley, the mate, was allowed to go home and seamen Gordon Parrot and Moses Janes were put up at the Kitchener Hotel.

It took some time for the hospitalized men to recover, but eventually, they, too were allowed to go home. For Captain Janes and all the crew members, the last voyage of the *A.B. Barteau* was one they would never forget.

A HARROWING SEA VOYAGE

The Loss of the Schooner Annie M. Parker in 1923

IN THE LATE FALL OF 1923, the two-masted schooner, *Annie M. Parker,* under the command of Captain Hollett, sailed from Burin for Oporto with a load of dried fish. They had a quick passage across the Atlantic and arrived safely at Oporto, where they landed their fish and took on a load of salt for their home port of Burin.

After his ship had been given a clean bill of health by the Portuguese port authorities, Captain Hollett set sail on the return voyage to Burin. Eleven days out of Oporto, the mate came down with the dreaded smallpox. With little medical knowledge or medical supplies, Captain Hollett and his men did all they could with their limited resources to help the stricken mate. However, he gradually became worse and it became clear that he was badly in need of proper medical treatment.

Twenty-eight days out of Oporto, Cape Race was sighted and Captain Hollett hoped he would reach port in time to save the mate's life. However, it was not to be, for shortly after Cape Race had been sighted a dreadful northeasterly gale sprang up with winds of hurricane force. The *Annie M. Parker* was dismasted in the storm and blown far out to sea, where, under the constant battering of the waves, she became a drifting, leaking derelict.

Captain Hollett and his men were now in the terrible position of being stranded on a sinking ship with a man dying of smallpox. For two days the schooner was tossed about by the huge waves, with the captain and crew expecting each moment to be their last. Then, on the third day, the wind and waves abated and the their distress signal was seen by the Dutch steamer SS *Hollander*. The steamer came alongside and, after much difficulty, managed to transfer the men from the *Annie M. Parker* to the *Hollander*.

Three days after their rescue, the mate died and had to be buried at sea. The members of the rescued crew had been placed in isolation on the *Hollander*, and after the mate's death, three of them also developed smallpox. On their arrival in Rotterdam, Holland, the men were placed in hospital. Captain Hollett and the cook, Mr. Haben were placed in quarantine, but did not develop the disease.

When the quarantine period was over, Captain Hollett and the cook were permitted to return home. The other three crew members had to remain in hospital. The captain and cook travelled to Liverpool, and from there took passage on one of the Cunard liners to Halifax.

They travelled from Halifax to Sydney and made connections with the SS *Kyle* to return home to Newfoundland. Captain Hollett was loud in praise of the Dutch people who did everything they could to help them in their hour of need. He was not so complimentary to the English authorities in Liverpool. They, he found, had little or no knowledge of Newfoundland. The other three crew members recovered and were returned to Newfoundland at a later date.

STRUCK BY LIGHTNING

The Wreck of the Schooner Inspiration, November 4, 1924

THE SCHOONER *INSPIRATION* was a 326-ton schooner built at Conquerale Bank, Nova Scotia, in 1917. In 1922, she was purchased by the St. John's firm of Messrs. James Baird Ltd. for the foreign trade.

The schooner, under the command of Captain William Doyle, left Pernambuco in ballast on September 21, 1924 for her home port of St. John's. The weather was good and the ship was making a good passage until October 27 when about 3:00 A.M. in the latitude 41 north and longitude 51 west they ran into a fierce thunder and lightning storm with heavy rain and high seas. The schooner was weathering the storm very well, when a bolt of lightning struck the foremast, split it into three pieces and carried away the main topmast and jib-boom.

When the foremast gave way it blocked up the mizzen and main rigging. The work of clearing away the wreckage was begun, but had not been half completed when the turnbuckle in the mizzen rigging broke, and the mizzen-mast cracked off at the deck. Going over the side it carried the mainmast head with it.

Luckily, the wind was moderate when the damage occurred, but it was no easy task for the crew of the *Inspiration* to clear away the wreckage. It took four hours of back-breaking work to cut away the tangled mass of wire ropes and rigging. To make it more difficult, the wind began to increase just after daylight, and soon reached hurricane-force.

In the middle of this storm the crew had to put up rigging, place stops to the stump of the mainmast and try to set up jury sails. This took them the better part of two days. When it was finished and the ship was again under sail, Captain Doyle surveyed the scene and decided that there was no way he could continue the return voyage to St. John's with only a fragment of the ship's original canvas. He decided to put back to Barbados to have the ship repaired before continuing the voyage.

In the meantime, they ran into a west-northwest gale and then on the twenty-ninth and thirtieth of October, light winds and heavy seas prevailed and the ship made little progress toward Barbados. On Saturday, November 1, the SS *City of Aukland* was sighted. Seeing the dismasted *Inspiration* with her jury rig of sail, the steamer came alongside and offered to take off the crew. However Captain Doyle said they were still in hope of making Barbados under their own sail. He did ask the captain of the *Aukland* to report his position to James Baird Ltd. at St. John's.

Sunday, November 2, the weather became stormy, when a heavy breeze blew up from the northwest and the dismasted schooner was once again battered by heavy seas. The storm continued all Sunday and into Monday, and all Captain Doyle could do was heave to and try to ride out the storm. During Monday night, the high seas carried away the rudder braces. The rudder then smashed through its case and the ship began to leak badly and take on water faster than the pumps could clear it out. The situation of Captain Doyle and his six-man crew was now desperate, as it was clear the ship could not remain afloat, for long even with the pumps working full time.

As soon as daylight broke on November 4, they hoisted distress signals and their prayers were answered when, at 7:00 A.M., the Royal Mail steamer, SS *Cardiganshire* hove into sight. Seeing the distress signals, Captain Faulkner of the SS *Cardinganshire* came as close to the damaged ship as possible. He then launched a lifeboat under the command of Chief Officer Avern and manned by eight sailors, They went to take off the crew of the *Inspiration*.

Getting alongside the schooner was a very difficult task, for the seas were still running high, and the rescue crew risked swamping their boat. Finally, at 8:30 A.M., all seven men were in the lifeboat, but not before they had shipped two feet of water. It took two hours to make it back to the rescue ship.

Captain Faulkner and his crew did everything to make the rescued crew comfortable and took them to Liverpool, England, where the *Cardiganshire* was bound. They arrived there on November 11, and were taken to the Sailor's Home until their passage could be arranged for Newfoundland. The mate of the *Inspiration,* Mr. Noseworthy, had to be hospitalized and could not return with his fellow crew members on the SS *Digby,* which brought Captain Doyle and the others back to Newfoundland.

They arrived back in St. John's on December 4, just one month after they had been rescued from the sinking *Inspiration*. Captain Doyle and his crew were loud in their praise of the treatment they received from the captain and crew and passengers of the SS *Cardiganshire* and the officials of the Sailor's Home in Liverpool.

Captain Doyle lost all his clothing and nautical instruments and his crew lost all their belongings in the shipwreck.

Captain Doyle also denied a report that had appeared in the English papers, that the *Inspiration* had run short of provisions. He stated that the ship had plenty of provisions and could have sailed for at least another month before running short of anything.

A JINXED SHIP

The Loss of the Elly (Amy Stella)

March 2, 1926

THE *ELLY,* A 150-TON TERN SCHOONER, was built in Holland in 1913, and was later purchased by the Fishermen's Union Trading Company, Port Union. In

December, 1925, the *Elly,* under the command of Captain Wes Green, left Port Union with a cargo of dried fish for Brazil. After a good voyage she arrived at Pernambucto and landed her cargo. As well, while she was at Brazil, the ship's name was changed from *Elly* to *Amy Stella.* The crew didn't like the changing of names and grumbled among themselves, for there is an old seafaring tradition that to do so is to invite disaster. It was perhaps an omen of what was to happen on the return voyage.

The *Elly,* now the *Amy Stella,* left Pernambuco in ballast in early January on her return voyage to Newfoundland. She was making good time with favourable winds until she ran into the northeast trade winds which were very strong. For several days the wind and waves battered the *Elly* and most of her sails were blown away. The damage was so severe that the *Elly* had to put into Barbados for repairs.

On February 2, 1926, the schooner left Barbados and made a good voyage until February 23, when a storm blew up, accompanied by heavy seas, which swept her decks fore and aft. The storm continued to batter the *Elly* and, as the ship neared the Newfoundland coast, it grew worse. Then at 2:00 A.M. on March 2, just one month after leaving Barbados, the *Elly* struck on the shoals in Golden Bay, near Cape St. Mary's.

At first it was decided to stay on the ship until daylight, when they could better assess their chances of refloating the schooner. However, it was soon apparent that the ship was a total loss and, about an hour after they struck, it was decided to abandon ship.

It was no easy task to launch a boat in such heavy seas, but the men succeeded in getting away from the ship without capsizing in the waves breaking against the stranded vessel. At first they tried to make the nearby community of Branch, but had to abandon this plan, as the seas were running too high, and even breaking over the cliffs along the coast. In fact, the lifeboat was constantly shipping water and the men who were not rowing had to bail for dear life with their hats and caps to keep her from being swamped.

Not being able to make it into Branch, it was decided to try and land at Admiral's Beach, near Colinet. However, once again, it proved to be too dangerous to effect a landing.

Undaunted, though wet and cold from the constant seas breaking over them, the men kept their boat head on to the seas, and kept on rowing in toward the bottom of St. Mary's Bay.

At dusk they came in sight of a place called Red Lane Cove. There were breakers ahead and, as none of the men were familiar with the place they didn't know how difficult it might be to land. However, now they felt it a case of do or die and they made for the breakers, hoping for the best. With a sail set on the boat and rowing with all their might the men ran over the reef and into the breakers.

They were tossed about pretty badly but managed to get on some rocks and were able to make their way to shore. As it was raining very hard, they decided to make a shelter out of the boat's sail and oars and wait until morning to find a community. Here, huddled together, the seven shipwrecked men spent a terrible night. To make matters worse, just before dawn, the wind changed and the temperature fell to below freezing. The men had their wet clothes frozen to their bodies and several suffered frostbitten hands and feet.

When dawn broke they found a lobster fisherman's shack near by and took shelter there. They had no fire or food, but it did protect them from the elements. In the afternoon the captain and boatswain left for Cape Dog. Here they found a hunting shack with rifles and utensils. Shortly after they got to the shack, a man who was hunting on the barrens brought them some food, and then led them to the community of North Harbour, St. Mary's Bay, where they were warmly welcomed by the citizens of that community.

As soon as Captain Green and his companion had told their story, Peter and John Power made ready to leave to carry food to the crew members still in the lobster man's shack at Red Lane Cove. They tramped the nine miles over ponds and through snow to the shack, which they reached at around 4:00 P.M. They lit a fire in the stove and gave the starving crew food and warm drinks. As it was now too dark to return to North Harbour, the two Powers stayed with the crew that night.

The next morning, two more men from North Harbour arrived and, with the help of the seamen, they launched the lifeboat and rowed back to North Harbour, where they arrived around midday on Friday. The shipwrecked crew were taken in by various members of the community and were well looked after.

They rested up until Sunday and then they left to join the train at Whitbourne. The people of North

Harbour took them by horse and catamarans to the train station. Here they caught the express to go to their homes. Captain Green came on to St. John's and reached home March 12, after a most harrowing experience.

Both Captain Green and his crew members were loud in their praise of the people of North Harbour and Colinet, who went out of their way to help them.

The news of the loss of the *Amy Stella* (*Elly*) was a serious financial blow to the Fishermen's Union Trading Company, as it marked the third vessel belonging to that firm lost in a three month period.

LOST ON A HOMEWARD VOYAGE

The Cecil J. Abandoned in Mid-Ocean

March 22, 1926

THE *CECIL J.* WAS A WOODEN three-masted vessel of 260 tons. She was built in 1913 at Shelburne, Nova Scotia for Captain Abram Kean, the famous Newfoundland sealing captain. The ship measured 115.2 feet long with a 28.2 beam and a depth of 11.3 feet.

On or about November 18, 1925, the *Cecil J.* loaded a cargo of fish at Herring Neck for the Spanish market. She had a pleasant if slow trip across the Atlantic and arrived at Seville, Spain on Old Christmas Day, 1926. The ship unloaded her cargo and then on February 28, 1926 sailed in ballast for Newfoundland.

The master of the *Cecil J.* was Captain Burden. The mate was Malcolm Penny, the bosun was William Butt and there were two sailors, Samuel Cole and Nicholas Shanahan.

The return voyage across the Atlantic proved to be very stormy, and heavy seas damaged the ship's stern and started a number of leaks in the vessel. Soon, it became evident that the pumps could not clear the vessel and the *Cecil J.* was sinking. It now became a race against time whether a rescue ship would appear in time to save them or they would go down with their ship. It was still blowing a raging gale, and Captain Burden and his crew knew that even if a rescue ship arrived, it would be no easy task to man a lifeboat in such rough seas.

On March 22, their sinking spirits were raised when a steamer the SS *War Divan,* was sighted. They sent up distress signals and the *War Divan* came to their rescue. It was difficult getting the shipwrecked crew to the steamer, but at last all were on board without any mishap. Before leaving the battered hulk of the *Cecil J,* the crew set fire to her so that she wouldn't become a menace to shipping.

On March 23, Captain Burden sent a message to Halifax, reporting that The *Cecil J.* had been abandoned and set on fire in latitude 41.04 north, longitude 37.40 west. Captain and crew were safe on board the SS *War Divan*.

The *War Divan* landed the destitute crew at Lisbon, Portugal, and then continued on her own voyage. From the Lisbon port, the shipwrecked Newfoundlanders were sent to Southampton and then took passage on the SS *Rosalind* to Halifax. From Halifax the shipwrecked crew arrived back in Newfoundland on April 30.

The men had little to say about their harrowing experience, and left St. John's for their homes in Carbonear and Harbour Grace.

The loss of the *Cecil J.* and her cargo of fish was a heavy blow to Captain Abram Kean's shipping business.

ABANDONED NEAR THE COAST OF SPAIN

The Schooner, Olive Moore Abandoned, November 8, 1930

IN THE FALL OF 1930, THE SCHOONER, *Olive Moore,* commanded by Captain F.J. Pine, left Salmon Bight, Labrador for Malaga, Spain. The ship carried 5,000 quintals of fish for the Spanish market. The cargo was owned by A.E. Hickman of St. John's.

The *Olive Moore* was a 189-ton, tern schooner built at Liverpool, Nova Scotia for the Carbonear firm of J & F. Moore in 1920. In 1930 she was owned by her captain, F.J. Pine, who chartered his vessel to various Newfoundland fish firms. The schooner had crossed the Atlantic many times and handled well, even in stormy weather.

The voyage from Salmon Bight to Malaga was uneventful until November 5, when the *Olive Moore* was about 500 miles off the coast of Spain. Here, a sudden hurricane swept over the ocean and the *Olive Moore* was directly in its path. The high winds stripped away her canvas and tore the foremast right out of the schooner. As well, huge waves battered the hull, putting so much strain on her timbers that the hull was, in places, wrenched open and water began to pour into the ship.

Immediately the crew manned the pumps and pumped for their lives. However, despite this, the water kept gaining in the hold and it was now only a matter of keeping the schooner afloat until help arrived. When the cargo of dry fish began to get water-logged and, fearing the extra weight would drag the *Olive Moore* under, Captain Pine gave the order to jettison cargo.

As the winds were still high and the seas rough, it was no easy task to lift the fish from the hold and throw it overboard. But with every extra pound a matter of life and death, the crew did manage to get clear of a large quantity of fish. This gave the *Olive Moore* more buoyancy and, with the pumps being manned twenty-four hours a day there was some hope of staying afloat until they met up with a passing steamer.

Three days passed and,despite the constant working of the pumps, the schooner settled farther and farther down in the water. When day dawned on November 8, Captain Pine and his crew knew that rescue must come soon or it would be too late.

Then, when hope was just about gone, the Italian freighter *Montello* came into view. Would she see and respond to their distress signals? Captain Pine and his weary crew hoped and prayed. Then a cheer went up from the *Olive Moore,* the *Montello* had changed course and was coming towards them.

The *Montello* had come to their rescue, but getting the men off the sinking schooner was no easy task, as the waves were still running high, and the wind was blowing at gale force. The *Montello* manoeuvred as close as she could to the stricken ship, and then poured oil to smoothen the rough seas between them.

Captain Pine and his crew then launched their lifeboat and,shielded by the freighter, managed to row to her side,where they were taken on board. The weather was so bad that the freighter had to heave to, to ride out the gale.

Three hours later, Captain Pine and his crew watched the *Olive Moore* disappear beneath the waves. It was a sobering thought to the crew of the lost ship that another three hours would have seen them adrift in the North Atlantic in their lifeboat at the mercy of the storm.

The *Montello* took Captain Pine and his five-man crew,composed of F. Dwyer, mate, Walter Hodder, C. Warren, H. Parrott and James Moore to Gibraltar. From there they travelled to London and took passage on an ocean liner to Halifax. At Halifax they joined the SS *Nova Scotia* for their return to Newfoundland.

Luckily for Captain Pine and A.E Hickman & Company, insurance was carried on both the schooner and the cargo. The crew members lost all their belongings, but considered themselves lucky to be alive after such a close call.

A MISTAKEN CHRISTMAS MESSAGE
The Loss of the John W. Miller, December 30, 1930

ON NOVEMBER 26, 1930, the schooner *John W. Miller* left the port of St. John's with a full cargo of dried fish for Brazil. The vessel was under the command of Captain Cyril Horwood and carried a crew of six seamen. The first two days out of St. John's they had a fair wind and on November 28 were in the vicinity of the "Virgin Rocks" on the Grand Banks. It was here that the beginning of a four week voyage of terror and misery was to begin.

The weather, which had been good up to this date, suddenly changed, and a great storm sprang up and swept the Grand Banks. The *John W. Miller* was caught directly in the eye of the storm.

Captain Horwood was an experienced master, and when the storm broke he gave orders to reef the sails, batten down the hatches, and ride out the gale. However, so fierce were the gale force winds that they ripped the canvas from the ship and the mountainous seas tore away her rudder. This left the *John W. Miller* a drifting hulk, totally at the mercy of the elements.

With the ship totally out of control, the only hope for Captain Horwood and his crew was that their distress signals would be seen by a passing ship that would come to their rescue. It wasn't long before a steamer was sighted and the captain and crew of the

John W. Miller signalled. The ship either did not see or did not chose to respond, and kept on her way. Seven times this was to happen, and in the meantime, the rudderless derelict drifted farther and farther out into the North Atlantic.

Christmas Day came after they had been drifting for three weeks, but it brought little cheer to the men on board. The passing steamers which did not come to their assistance sapped their courage and they felt doomed. Hope revived again on the afternoon of Christmas Day when another steamer appeared on the horizon. Once again the men on the *John H. Miller* desperately signalled for help.

Then came the cruelest blow of all. The crew on the steamer mistook their signal for Christmas greetings and signalled back "happy returns," and went merrily on their way. It was a very miserable Christmas for all hands on the derelict.

The vessel had now drifted to about 500 miles southwest of the Azores and, on December 30, another steamer was sighted. Once again, but with little hope of rescue, the distress signals were sent up, but this time luck was on their side. The steamer acknowledged their signals and came to their rescue.

The steamer turned out to be the *Wido*, a freighter of German registry. She came alongside and took Captain Horwood and his other six crew members off their disabled craft. The steamer then landed them at Colon in Cuba, and from there they went on to New York.

From New York they took passage on the SS *Rosalind* and arrived in St. John's on February 2, 1931. The shipwrecked men praised the crew of the rescue ship for the kindness shown them, and the other agencies that had arranged their passage home. Besides Captain Cyril Horwood, the crew members were John Green, William Laing, Joseph Clarke, Frank Rogers, Theodore Pike and William Kennedy. The men had managed to save most of their personal belongings before leaving the ill-fated *John W. Miller*.

A DARING OCEAN RESCUE

Neptune 11 Abandoned in Mid-Ocean, January 14, 1935

ON DECEMBER 29, 1934, the seventy-eight-ton, schooner-rigged, auxiliary vessel *Neptune 11,* left Harbour Buffett, Placentia Bay, with a full load of 3,080 quintals of dried fish for the European market. The cargo was jointly owned by Crosbie's of St. John's and W.W. Wareham of Harbour Buffett. The schooner was skippered by Captain Heber Keeping of Grand Bank and his crew consisted of John Keeping from Hr. Breton and John Tizzard, Matthew English, John Dolimount and Frank Thornhill all of Grand Bank.

They had only just cleared Harbour Buffett when they immediately ran into bad weather. Strong winds from the northeast and huge seas put a heavy strain on the ship, but everything went well until January 5, 1935.

At this time, John Tizzard, the cook, reported to the captain that he could hear water sloshing about under the floor of the forecastle. His report was confirmed by

John Keeping, the mate who had also been alerted by the cook.

Immediately, the captain and crew undertook a search of the vessel to find the source of the leak. They found that she was leaking near the stem, but these leaks were so small that they did not explain the presence of water under the forecastle floor. The captain then decided that the leak must be in the bottom of the ship and ordered the pumps manned. For the next nine days the crew did pump duty, going twenty-four hours a day.

To make matters worse for Captain Keeping and his crew the weather continued bad, the northeast gales continued and the sea was very rough. This continued until Sunday, January 13, when the winds changed and became southerly. However, all this time the vessel was rolling and pitching and under great strain. As well, giant waves washed over her decks and to add, to the fears of the captain and crew, the water in the hold continued to rise, despite the constant manning of the pumps. In fact, by January 13, the water had risen to four feet among the ship's cargo of dried fish. This now became waterlogged and the extra weight made the ship unmanageable.

By now, the crew were near exhaustion from trying to work the ship in the stormy weather and manning the pumps. It also became apparent that their chances of making port, any port, were indeed slim. They knew the vessel was doomed and their only hope of survival was to be rescued by a passing steamer.

On Sunday evening they saw a steamer, but she was so far away they didn't even bother to hoist their distress signals, and she passed from sight. Then, the wind came up again, and in that howling gale, Captain Keeping and his crew fought for their lives. It took all their skill and strength to keep the waterlogged craft afloat. Exhausted and cold, but with sheer will and determination, they managed to weather the gale.

Unknown to them, the same gale that was threatening their lives was also bringing them help; for caught up in the same storm was the 4,000-ton oil-tanker *M.M. Wellfield*. This ship was trying to batter her way from Curacao to Purfleet, but when the storm increased in intensity she was forced to lie to, not far from the waterlogged *Neptune 11*. During the night the *Wellfield* drifted off course and when the winds died down in the morning she was headed towards the *Neptune 11*.

On Monday morning, January 14, the storm battered captain and crew of the *Neptune 11* saw the *M.M. Wellfield* approaching. They were all in agreement that their only hope of survival was to abandon the waterlogged *Neptune 11*, and the appearance of the oil tanker seemed a gift of Providence. They began to signal for assistance and were soon overjoyed to see their call answered and the tanker change course to approach them.

However, their troubles were not yet over, for the seas had not abated sufficiently to allow the tanker to come alongside. There was nothing to do but launch a dory and row to the rescue ship.

As it was not safe for all hands to go together in the dory, four men, English, Dolimount, Thornhill and the mate made the first trip. Dolimount and the mate were put aboard the tanker and English and Thornhill went back for Captain Keeping and Tizzard, the cook. It was rough going but they made it back to the tanker. Before leaving his ship, Captain Keeping set fire to the *Neptune 11* to prevent her becoming a navigational hazard to other shipping.

As soon as the rescue was complete the M.M. *Wellfield* continued her voyage and landed the shipwrecked crew at Purfleet, England. From here they travelled to London by train and in London were looked after by the Shipwrecked Mariners' Society. On January 29, they signed on as crew members of the SS *Philip T. Dodge,* and after delivering a load of coal to Wales, returned to St. John's. The men returned home by the SS *Portia,* thankful they had been able to cheat the sea of its intended victims.

A TOUGH BATTLE WITH THE SEA

The Wreck of the Dazzle, January 11, 1940

THE NINETY-ONE-TON, three-masted Newfoundland fishing schooner *Dazzle,* with a load of 700 tons of fish for the Lisbon market, was twenty-two days out of St. John's when she ran into a terrible northeast gale. The wind and the waves tore at the ship and carried away her mainsail. It also smashed her bulwarks aft by the mizzen-mast and loosened the rudder posts. This caused some leaking, and the five-man crew had to man the pumps constantly. On Christmas Day the storm still raged and they feasted on coffee and hard tack. The storm continued and the winds increased to hurricane force, with fearsome waves battering the *Dazzle*.

The water reached the cargo and they lost one of their fresh water tanks. Then found it impossible to keep the salt water out of their other tank. The wind increased and they lost the foresail. For the next forty-eight hours they ran under the jib.

On New Year's Day, a halyard was carried away and a sea broke over the schooner's deck, taking the binnacle. It also smashed the after hatch and flooded the cabin.

As soon as the storm subsided a little the captain made his decision to abandon ship. He told the crew to set all possible sails and he set the vessel's course for the steamship lanes. As well, a distress signal was hoisted to attract the attention of any ship in the neighbourhood. In the meantime the men manned the pumps day and night but the water in the hold gained steadily. The only hope of survival was that a passing ship would rescue them.

Their situation was growing desperate, when at 1:00 P.M. on January 11, 1940, their prayers were answered. A ship sighted their distress signal and responded. It was the Italian steamship, *Pietro Orseolo* that had sighted their distress signal and come to their assistance. The crew were taken off the *Dazzle* and, to prevent her becoming a threat to shipping, she was set on fire. The Italian ship then carried on to New York. The British consulate in New York arranged for the shipwrecked crew to stay at the

Seamen Church Institute on 25 South Street while arrangements were made for their return to Newfoundland.

Later, Captain John Murphy and his mate Uriah Gilbert paid tribute to their crew, who had worked so hard and long to save the ship. They had battled tremendous gales and tried everything, but in the end they lost and the ocean claimed the *Dazzle*.

NO ONE LEFT TO TELL THE TALE

Ships Lost In the Foreign Trade With No Survivors

THROUGHOUT Newfoundland's long maritime history in the foreign trade, which until 1949, included ships trading to Canadian ports, many ships have come to grief. From some, come tales of battling the elements and heroic rescues at sea; from others there is nothing but broken wreckage and battered bodies to tell the story of the men who went down with their ships. For others there are no tidings at all. They disappeared during a voyage and nothing was ever known of what happened to them. The following are but a few of the many ships that never returned.

SPRAY

On May 4, 1869, the St. John's newspapers reported the loss of the brigantine *Spray*, owned by Job Brothers. The

Spray was on a return voyage from Alicante, Spain, with a load of salt when she struck on Puffin's Point, Torbay, on Friday night, April 30. It was very foggy at the time and blowing a gale. What happened to the ship is unknown as there were no survivors. The captain of the *Spray* was a young Englishman named Furze and she carried a crew of nine men, six of them Newfoundlanders. On Saturday, May 1, the steamer *Diamond* went to the scene of the wreck, but nothing was visible except the topmast head which was above water.

On June 4, 1869 the body of Joseph Parr, second mate on the *Spray,* was picked up at Torbay and was interred there. On June 29, another body was recovered from a cod seine. Identification was difficult but it was believed to be the body of a man named Carroll, one of the seamen lost in the wreck of the *Spray*.

ISABELLA

On February 22, 1881, the brigantine, *Isabella* owned by Job Brothers, disappeared in St. Mary's Bay. The ship was engaged in the foreign trade and was returning from a voyage to Brazil under the command of Captain H.G. Quick. There were no survivors from the shipwreck. The men who perished in this disaster were:

Henry G. Quick,	master from England
William Tucker,	mate from England
Patrick McGibbon,	bosun, from Ireland
James Hooper,	cook and steward, country of origin unknown
Joseph Riding,	seaman " " " "

John Anderson,	seaman	" " " "
John Kelly,	seaman	Newfoundland
Robert Parsley,	seaman	Newfoundland

N.P. CHRISTIAN

This schooner from Bay Roberts disappeared with all hands on a voyage to North Sydney, February, 1895.

SWALLOW

On January 18, 1909, the authorities at St. John's were informed of the loss of the schooner *Swallow* in a gale at Long Island Sound, New York. There were no survivors. The schooner was taking a load of herring from Green Bay to the New York markets. She had loaded in Green Bay and then put into St. John's where a new captain and one new crew member were taken on board. The new captain, Frank Morris took the ship's compass to have it adjusted, but was told if the compass was off the trouble was on the ship, where the compass was fastened to the binnacle. Captain Morris refused to wait to have this problem corrected and sailed with a faulty compass.

The *Swallow* was an eighty-five-ton schooner built in 1907 and owned by C.F. Taylor. The hull of the ill-fated schooner was found a mile west of Oak Island, New York Sound. Besides Frank Morris, her captain, the ship carried a crew of five. Three of the lost crew members were mate, Charles Harmish of Liverpool, Nova Scotia, cook, William Rice, of Pilley's Island and seaman Elih Pattey, of St. Anthony. The other two crew members were foreigners whose names were not known to Captain Daggett, who owned the load of herring. No bodies were recovered from this wreck.

ARKANSAS

On December 22, 1911, the schooner *Arkansas* sailed from Grand Bank for Gibraltar with a load of fish for the foreign market. The schooner was under the command of Captain Devoe and carried a crew of five. She was never seen again after leaving Grand Bank and it was believed she foundered in one of the gales that swept the North Atlantic after her departure. No wreckage or bodies were ever recovered.

SS ERMA

The SS *Erma* sailed from Glasgow, Scotland for St. John's, Newfoundland on February 28, 1912. The steamer had. besides her regular crew, the shipwrecked crew of the *Aureola* who had been rescued from their sinking ship in the North Atlantic on January 27, 1912. The total ship's company numbered fifty-one, none of whom were ever seen again and no wreckage nor bodies were ever recovered.

RELIANCE

A schooner owned by Templeton & Company of Bonavista lost with all hands in the winter of 1912, on a return voyage from Naples, Italy.

DOROTHY LOUISE

Schooner lost with all hands on a return voyage from Oporto in the winter of 1912.

SS BEVERLY

Steamship left Harbour Grace with a load of fish for the European market on January 22, 1918, was never heard from again. She was presumed to have foundered with all hands in a winter gale.

DOUGLAS ADAMS

Schooner on a return voyage from Lisbon to Twillingate, lost with all hands after leaving Lisbon on September 5, 1921.

PERCY WELLS

Vessel left New York with a load of hard coal for St. John's. Believed to have foundered with all hands in a storm on October 2, 1921.

ROY BRUCE

The *Roy Bruce* was owned by R.F. Hollett of Burin, who was also master. The wreckage of this vessel was found in mid-Atlantic with her hull cut in two. The crew were never heard from again. The vessel was seventy-five days out from Spain on a return voyage to Burin when the wreckage was discovered by the SS *Huronia* on May 15, 1924.

PEAR EVELINE

The schooner, *Pear Eveline*, Fennel, master, lost with all hands on a voyage to Oporto in the winter of 1929.

A.V. Conrad. Tern Schooner. Built at Lahave, NS in 1908. 178 gross tons, length 192 feet. Owned by Hickmans of St. John's. Lost in the Mid-Atlantic in 1921. On a return voyage from Cadiz, salt-laden, she lost her rudder. After drifting for several days, the crew were rescued by a passing vessel.

Ada. Brigantine. Built by master ship builder Michael Kearney on the site of the main Post Office on Water Street in St. John's.

Alembic. Brigantine. Built in 1894. 254 net tons. Purchased by Job Brothers in 1915 designed as a tanker, perhaps the first in Newfoundland. Lost in 1934 in the area of Cape Freels South coming from Montreal.

Amorel. Tern Schooner. Built in Harbour Grace in 1918. 378 net tons. Owned by C. Tessier and later sold to French interest in 1921.

Antoinette. Schooner. Built at Plymouth in 1905. 119 gross tons, length 94 feet. Owned by Munn's of Harbour Grace. She was lost after departing Patras, Greece for Newfoundland in 1914. Her and the crew were never heard from again.

Ariceen. Tern Schooner. Built at Liverpool, NS in 1917. 416 gross tons. Owned by W. Ashbourne of Twillingate. She was lost in Twillingate Harbour in 1921. The vessel was driven ashore where she finally broke up.

Asquth. Tern Schooner. Built in Bridgewater, NS in 1916. 271 net tons. Owned by A.E. Hickman of St. John's. Lost on a voyage from Seville.

Atlanta. Built at Charlottetown, PEI in 1864 by James White. Sold to Azariah Munden of Brigus, NL in 1865. Broken-up at Harbour Grace, NL in October 1900.

Beatrice. Brigantine. Built in England in 1901. 128 gross tons, length 91 feet. Owned by James Rorke of Carbonear. Lost with all crew in 1911 after leaving Cadiz for St. John's with a cargo of salt.

Benevolence. Schooner. Owned by George M. Barr of St. John's. Lost at St. Pierre in 1919.

Bianca. Tern Schooner. Built in Liverpool, NS in 1917. 313 net tons. Owned by Bowrings. Abandoned on voyage to Gibraltar in 1919.

Callidora. Barquentine. Built at Portmadoc, Wales in 1901. 144 gross tons, length 103 feet. Owned by James Rorke of Carbonear. Lost by fire in Carbonear Harbour in 1915. The vessel was a well-known trader to European posts.

Cape Race. Tern Schooner. Built in Liverpool, NS in 1918. 378 gross tons, length 127 feet. Owned by R.G. Bemsione of St. John's. Lost near St. Shotts in 1932. She was one of the largest Newfoundland vessels employed in the fish trade.

Cecil Junior. Tern Schooner. Built in Shelburne, NS in 1918. 260 gross tons, length 115 feet. Owned by A. Kean of St. John's. She was lost in the Mid-Atlantic in 1926 after returning from Cadiz was a cargo of salt.

Champion. Brigantine. Built at Morton's Harbour, NL in 1885. 89 gross tons, length 73 feet. Owned by Monroe of St. John's. Her registry was closed in 1933. She was a typical Newfoundland schooner built for the fish and coastal trade.

Clio. Barquentine. Built in Appledore, England in 1895. Owned by John Rorke of Carbonear. She was lost with all hands in 1985 returning home from Valencia with a cargo of salt.

Clutha. Brigantine. Built in Harbour Grace in 1841. 170 gross tons, length 89 feet. Owned by John Munn of Harbour Grace. She was broken up at Harbour Grace in 1854. The vessel was mostly employed operating between Newfoundland and England.

Clutha. Barquentine. Built in Ardossan, Scotland in 1881. 244 gross tons, length 125 feet. Owned by William P. Munn of Harbour Grace. It was lost in heavy ice trying to reach St, Johns in 1924. It was the last square-rigged sailing ships out of St. John's.

Corisande. Barquentine. Built at Devonshire in 1873. Owned by Baine Johnston of St. John's. Lost near Devil's Chimney (Southern Shore) in 1894. Bob Bartlett was a seaman on this vessel when she was lost.

Dahlia. Brigantine. Built in Devon in 1873. 127 net tons. Owned by L.L. Ester. She was lost coming from the South.

Dorothy. Topsail Schooner. Built at Portadoc, Wales in 1891. 143 gross tons, length 92 feet. Owned by J. Greaves of St. John's. She was lost in 1905 when the vessel collided with another in the Strait of Gibraltar.

Dorothy Duff. Tern Schooner. Built in Falmouth, NS in 1906. 186 gross tons, length 98 feet. Owned by William Duff of Carbonear. She was lost off the Spanish Coast near Valencia in 1917; the result of a German U-boat.

E.D. Bailey. Tern Schooner. Built in Lunenburg, NS in 1918. 203 gross tons, length 119 feet. Owned by Moores of Bay de Verde. She was lost off Brazil in 1924. The vessel was used extensively in the Carribean and Brazilian trade.

Elizabeth Fern. Tern Schooner. Built in Placentia in 1917. 296 net tons. Owed by Campbell and McKay. She was lost at Alicanta in 1920.

Ellie.

Emulator. Topsail Schooner. Built in Scotland in 1878. 170 gross tons, length 99 feet. Purchased by James Baird of St. John's in 1900. She was abandoned in the North Atlantic in 1902.

Evelyn. Tern Schooner. Built in Shellburne, NS in 1899. 181 gross tons. Length 107 feet. Owned by Crosby's of St. John's. In 1911 her registration was transferred to Barbados. She was lost at Isle Aux Bois on the Southern Shore in 1913.

Fayal. 573 tons. Lost entering Fogo from Portugal in September 1935.

Fleetwing. Barquentine. Built at Halls Bay (Notre Dame Bay) in 1857. 249 gross tons, length 131 feet. Owned by John Munn of Harbour Grace. In 1873 she was condemned as unseaworthy and sold.

Florence Swyer. Tern Schooner. Built in Charlottetown, NL in 1918. 157 net tons. Owned by A.E. Hickman of St. John's. Lost off Portugal in 1925.

General Byng. Tern Schooner. Built in Marystown in 1918. 169 net tons. Owned by P.L. Carr. Lost off Turkish Islands in 1928.

General Currie. Tern Schooner. Built in Grand Bank by Eli Harris in 1918. 195 gross tons, length 107 feet. Originally owned by Samuel Harris Limited her career was short. She was stranded and lost on St. Pierre and Miquelon in April 1922.

Glengarry. Brigantine. Built in Wallace, NS in 1864. 189 gross tons, length 105 feet. Owned by John Munn of Harbour Grace. She was off Cape Bonavista in 1878 while participating in the seal fishery.

Grace. Schooner. Built at Ispwich, England in 1883. 149 gross tons. Partly owned by Goodridge of St. John's. In 1895, she was lost with all hands sailing from Portugal with a load of salt.

Harriet. Barquentine. Built at Bridgeport, Dorset in 1873. 247 gross tons. Owned by Bowrings of St. John's. She was wrecked off Pouch Cove in 1882.

Humerist. Tern Schooner. Built in Trinity Bay in 1921. 141 net tons. Owned by Monroe Exporting Company. Lost in Placentia Bay in 1933.

Isobel Moore. Tern Schooner. Built in Liverpool, NS in 1920. Length 122 feet. Owned by J & F Moore and A.E. Hickman of St. John's. She was lost in Fortune Bay in 1930. The vessel was a sister ship of *Olive Moore* which was abandoned at sea the same year.

James O'Neill. Topsail Schooner. Built in Ireland in 1905. 98 gross tons. Owned by Munn's of Harbour Grace. In 1923, she was lost in the ice on a return voyage from Spain. The crew were rescued.

Jean. Tern Schooner. Built in Liverpool, NS in 1905. 190 net tons. Owned by Crosbie Company. She was sunk by a German Raider off Brazil in 1916.

Joan Hickman. Tern Schooner. Built in Charlottetown, NL in 1917. 295 net tons. She was lost off the Spanish coast in 1920.

John W. Miller. Tern Schooner. Built in Mahone Bay, NS in 1918. 301 gross tons, length 122 feet. Owned by J.C. Crosbie of St. John's. In 1930 she was lost while en route to South America with a cargo of salt fish.

Julia Johnson. Stranded at Seal Cove, Conception Bay in October, 1941.

Kate. Barquentine. Owned by Rork's of Carbonear. Operated for many years in the foreign trade.

Kinsman. Tern Schooner. Built at Charlottetown in 1919. 350 gross tons. Owned by A.E. Hickman of St. John's. She was lost off the Azores in 1922. It is assumed that the vessel was returning to Newfoundland with a cargo of salt.

Lord Nelson. Brigantine. Built in Halls Bat in 1857. 233 tons. Owned by J. Munn. She was condemned in Lisbon in 1873.

Luetta. Schooner. Built in Lunenburg, NS in 1895. 105 gross tons, length 96 feet. Owned by Kennedy and Snow of Carbonear and Twillingate. Lost at Herring Neck in 1921. The vessel was used mostly on the coast.

MV *Lutzen*. 339 net tons. Owned by Job Brothers. She was lost in February 1939 at Cape Cod on a voyage from St. John's to New York with a cargo of frozen blueberries.

Marie Louise H. Tern Schooner. Built at Charlottetown, NL in 1919. 383 net tons. Owned by A. E. Hickman of St. John's. She was abandoned in 1921 on a voyage from Portugal.

Mildred. Tern Schooner. Built at Lunenburg, NS in 1907. 199 gross tons, length 107 feet. Owned by G.M. Barr of St. John's. In 1918 she was lost on a return voyage from Portugal with a cargo of salt. It is presumed she went down somewhere in the Mid-Atlantic.

Baird's Wharf. Photo shows part of Baird Gordon's foreign vessels tied up at their premises at St. John's during the turn of the 19th century.

Mildred Pauline (formally *Herbert Fearn*). Tern Schooner. Built in Placentia in 1919. 325 net tons. Lost in the Mid-Atlantic in 1919.

Muriel. Topsail Schooner. Built at Devonshire in 1878. 165 gross tons, length 105 feet. Owned by John Rorke of Carbonear. In 1902, sailing from Alicante for St. John's, she was lost with all hands.

Nina L. Tern Schooner. Built at North Arm, Notre Dame Bay in 1907. 120 gross tons, length 88 feet. Owned by Crosbie's of St. John's. Lost in the Mid-Atlantic in 1911.

Nina L.C. Tern Schooner. Built at Port Union, NL in 1918. Length 137 feet. Owned by the Fisherman's Protective Union. Of Port Union. Returning to Newfoundland on her maiden voyage in 1919 she was lost somewhere in the Atlantic.

Novelty. Tern Schooner. Built at Port Granville, NS in 1910. 260 net tons, length 118 feet. Owned by George Barr of St. John's. She was lost in the eastern Atlantic in 1926. She was mostly employed in the transportation of fish.

Olinda. Barquentine. Built at Greenock in 1859. 262 gross tons, length 143 feet. Owned by Edwin Duder and later Baird and Gordon. Of St. John's. She was lost at Sable Island in 1886. The vessel traded to many areas over the world.

Olive Moore. Tern Schooner. Built in Liverpool in 1920. 158 net tons. Lost on voyage to Malaga in 1930. Sister ship of *Isobel Moore*.

Olwen. Tern Schooner. Built in Pembrook in 1886. 154 net tons. Owned by R. Munn. Lost on a return voyage from Teneriffe.

Phileen. Tern Schooner. Built in Dartmouth, NS in 1917. 195 gross tons, length 122 feet. Owned by A.S. Randell of St. John's as well as several others. She was abandoned in the Mid-Atlantic in 1919.

President Coaker. Tern Schooner. Built at Port Union in 1919. 260 net tons. Owned by the Fishermen's Protective Union. In 1924, returning from Brazil, she was lost at Seal Cove, Cape Race.

Procyon. Schooner. Built at Essex Maine in 1889. 114 gross tons, length 96 feet. Owned by William Munn of Harbour Grace. She was lost a Sandy Point, Labrador in 1914. Her main responsibility was loading fish for overseas markets.

Ruth Hickman. Tern Schooner. Built at Springdale, NL in 1918. 386 net tons. Owned by A.E. Hickman of St. John's. Lost near Dingle Bay, Ireland in 1920.

Shamrock. Brigantine. Built at Carbonear in 1885. 139 gross tons, length 93 feet. Owned by John Rorke of Carbonear. In 1901 she was lost by fire at Cape Harrison. The brig was mostly used for loading fish for overseas markets.

Sordello. Tern Schooner. Built in Botwood in 1919. g00 gross tons. She was lost in December 1919 in Seldom.

Stella. Tern Schooner. Built in Ayr, Scotland in 1893. 221 net tons. Owned by J. Baird. She was lost near Cuckholds Cove in 1920.

Sydney Smith. Topsail Schooner. Built at Portmadoc in 1985. 177 gross tons, length 102 feet. Owned by Ashbourne of Twillingate. She was lost with all crew in 1917. The vessel was ashore in Twillingate Harbour for five years when she was repaired and sent to Gibraltar with a cargo of fish.

Thomas Ridley. Brigantine. Built at Harbour Grace in 1841. 170 gross tons, length 89 feet. Owned by John Munn of Harbour Grace. The vessel was broken up at Harbour Grace in 1885. The brig was mostly employed operating between Newfoundland and England.

Tobeatic. Tern Schooner. Built in Liverpool, NS in 1908. 136 gross tons, length 102 feet. Owned by Petite and Hickman of St. John's. The vessel was abandoned in the Western Atlantic in 1914. She was primarily used as a banker and for transporting fish to market.

Union Jack. Tern Schooner. Built in Trinity Bay in 1918. 142 net tons. Owned by S.W. Monroe. The vessel was lost at Seldom in 1926.

W.H. Latimer. Brigantine. Built at Port Medway, NS in 1875. 194 gross tons, length 100 feet. Owned by Robert Bishop of St. John's. She was abandoned in the North Atlantic in 1884. The brig was mostly used in the West Indies trade.

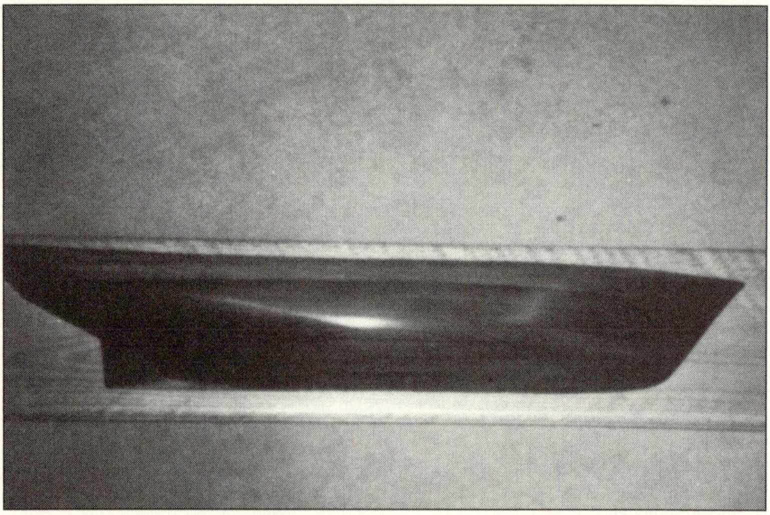

Workman. Tern Schooner. Built in Charlottetown, Bonavista Bay. Owned by A.E. Hickman of St. John's. She was lost in a dramatic collision when she was run down by a steamship near the Straits of Gibraltar in January 1922. As no photo of the vessel can be found, the image is her half model from which she was designed.

GLOSSARY

Alicante:	Spanish port on the Mediterranean Sea
Azores:	Islands in the Atlantic Ocean owned by Portugal
Able Seaman:	An experienced seaman competent to perform deck duties
About Ship:	To put a sailing vessel on the opposite tack
Admiralty Chart:	Charts produced by the Admiralty
Admiralty Court:	Special court where shipping cases are adjudicated
Aft:	The part of the ship near the stern
Brig:	Vessel with two masts and square sails
Boat's Painter:	Rope used to keep lifeboat alongside
Barque (Bark):	Sailing vessel with three or more masts rigged
Barquentine:	Vessel with three or more masts square-rigged forward
Bulwarks:	Wood erected around upper deck to prevent entry of the sea
Bowspit:	Spar projecting over stem
Backstays:	Ropes leading from mast to support mast against forward forces

Bahia:	Seaport in Brazil
Bilge:	Rounded part of ship's underwater hull
Ballast:	Heavy substances put in a vessel to improve stability
Back Ship:	To work vessel astern with sail or engine
Banker:	Cod fishing vessel on the Grand Banks
Bare Poles:	Mast with no sails
Beam Ends:	When a vessel is lying over on her sides
Bearing:	Direction an object lies from an observer
Cadiz:	Seaport in Spain
Canvas:	Refers to a vessel's sails
Cutwater:	Forward edge of the stem
Current:	Horizontal movement of current in the water
Dog Watch:	One of two hour watches from 4 to 8 to effect changes in watches
Dried Fish:	Cod fish salted and dried for market
Doldrums:	Windless zone along the Equator
Forecastle:	Crew's quarters

Foresail:	The foremost sail on a vessel with two sails
Figueras:	Seaport in Spain
Harness cask:	A large cask or tub with a rim cover, containing, a supply of salt meat for immediate use.
Hurricane Force:	Any wind over 60 knots
Heave To:	To bring a vessel in to wind and sea and stay in that postion
Helm:	Means by which a rudder is controlled
Helmsman:	Person steering the vessel
Icing Up:	Spray coming on board and freezing
In Ballast:	Said of a vessel when not carrying cargo
Jib-boom:	Boom projecting forward from bowsprite
Jury Rudder:	Makeshift rudder
Jonas:	A person on board a ship who coincides with misfortune
Logbook:	Book in which everything relating to the vessel is kept
Leeway:	Direction in which a vessel is forced off her course
Mizzen-mast:	The third mast from forward

Malaga:	A Spanish seaport on the Mediterranean sea
Magnetic Compass:	A compass which is influenced by Earth's magnetic field
Oporto:	A seaport in Portugal
Net Tons:	Relates to the cargo carrying space on board a ship
Puncheon:	A large cask of different capacities
Pernambuco:	A seaport in Brazil
Quadrant:	A nautical instrument for measuring altitudes
Reef:	A part of a sail between reef points
Snow Squall:	Intermittent snow and wind
Stanchion:	Vertical member supporting rails
Stem:	Bow rising from a vessel's keel
Tern:	Three-masted schooner
Sextant:	Instrument for measuring the angular distance between two objects: used at sea to measure the altitude of the sun, a star etc. to determine latitude and longitude.
Signal Flare:	Used to attract attention
Sao Paulo:	A seaport in Brazil

APPENDIX I

PARTIAL LIST OF NEWFOUNDLAND VESSELS LOST IN THE FOREIGN FISH TRADE

A.B. Barteau: 180-ton tern built in Minas Basin in 1909. Lost off Cape Race, 1923. Owner, A.S. Randell.

Accuracy: 72-ton schooner built in Shelburne, NS in 1929. Lost off Cape Cod, USA in 1936. Owner, Fortune Bay Shipping Company.

Ada Beard: 270-ton tern built in England, lost near Maccio in 1919. Owner, A.S. Randell.

Admiral Drake: 309-ton, tern, built in Shelburne, NS in 1916. Lost at Scatarie, NS in 1927. Owner, A.S. Randell.

Adriatic: 99-ton tern built in Bridgewater, NS in 1907. Lost at St. Lawrence, NL in 1918. Owner, A.E. Hickman.

Agnes P. Duff: 178-ton tern built in Laharve, NS in 1916. Lost at Renews Island NL In 1923. Owner, Campbell.

Albert Moulton: 110-ton schooner built in Burgeo, NL in 1902.Lost off Portugal on voyage to Oporto in 1919. Owner, R. Moulton.

Alembic: 254-ton auxiliary barque built in England in 1915. Lost at Cape Freels South, in 1936. Owner Job.

Alfreda May: 97-ton schooner built in Grand Bank, Nl. Lost in Atlantic on a voyage from Boston in 1901. Owner S. Patten.

Alhambia: 97-ton schooner built in Bridgewater, NS in 1918. Lost in Atlantic on voyage to Greece in 1938. Owner G. Noseworthy.

Alice M. Moulton: 197-ton tern built in Mahone Bay, NS in 1918. Lost in Atlantic at 44,20 N, latitude 39.20 W longitude on a voyage to Spain in 1919. Owner, R. Moulton.

Allan Rose: 98-ton schooner built at Belleoram, NL in 1928. Lost southeast of Cape Race in 1938. Owner, Harvey & Bell.

Allin C.Hollett: 95-ton schooner built in Marystown, NL. Lost in Atlantic, on a voyage from Oporto. Owner, T. Hollett.

Alsatian: 92-ton schooner built at Chester, NS in 1923. Lost in the Atlantic in 1935. Owner, S. Patten.

Amy B. Silver: 97-ton schooner built in Laharve, NS in 1912. Lost in the Atlantic on a voyage to Oporto in 1912. Owner, W. Tulk.

Amy Louise: 178-ton brig built in Prince Edward Island in 1897. Lost on a voyage from Pernambuco in 1910. Owner, Anglo Newfoundland Fish Company.

Anna Marcia: 272-ton tern built in Bridgewater, NS in 1914. Lost at Bordeaux, France, in 1919. Owner, Baine Johnston.

Annie E. Banks: 135-ton tern built in Laharve, NS in 1908. Lost in mid-Atlantic on a voyage from Oporto in 1914. Owner, Andrew King.

Annie M. Nardean: 132-ton schooner built in Port Daniel, PQ in 1918. Lost in the Atlantic on a voyage to Europe in 1921. Owner, J. Moulton.

Annie M. Parker: 100-ton schooner built in New Brunswick in 1908. Lost south of Cape Race, on a voyage from Oporto in 1918. Owner, Hollet's, Burn.

Annie Parker: 100-ton schooner built in Essex, MA in 1901. Lost in the Atlantic in 1924. Owner, Bay of Island Fisheries.

Annie Payer: 105-ton schooner built in Shelburne, NS in 1918. Lost in Atlantic on a voyage from Oporto in latitude 41.37 north, longitude 44.37 west, in 1924. Registered in St. John's.

Antoinette: 95-ton topsail schooner built in England in 1905. Lost on a voyage from Greece in 1915. Owner, W. Munn.

Arauconia: 120-ton schooner built in Placentia Bay, NL. Lost off Cape Breton in 1930. Owner, Campbell.

Arctic: 124-ton brig built in New Perlican, T.B. NL in 1880. Lost at St. Shott's in 1896. Owner, J. Munn.

Ariceen: 338-ton tern built in Liverpool, NS in 1917. Lost on a voyage to Twillingate in 1912. Owner, Ashbourne.

Ariel: 249-ton tern built at Liverpool, NS in 1900. Lost off Sydney NS in 1907. Owner, Bowrings.

Arkansas: 110-ton schooner built in the USA in 1903. Lost on a voyage to Gibraltar in 1911. Owner, G. Harris of Grand Bank.

Armistice: 198-ton tern built in Englee, NL in 1919. Lost on a voyage to Spain in 1922. Owner, A.E. Hickman.

Arnish: 466-ton tern built at St. Georges NL in 1917. Lost off Fogo NL in 1919. Owner, J. Fleet.

Arnold:	109-ton schooner built in Luneburg, NS in 1904. Lost on a voyage from Oporto in 1914.
Arthur W. Wight:	99-ton tern built in Luneburg, NS in 1904. Lost in the Atlantic on a voyage from San Andre in 1916. Owner, Horwood.
Artis:	97-ton schooner, built in Shelburn, NS in 1911. Lost in a collision in the Atlantic in 1917. Owner, P. Shea.
Ashler:	142-ton brig built in New Brunswick in 1871. Lost off Turks Island in 1880. Owner, L.Tessier.
Asquith:	271-ton tern built in Bridgewater, NS in 1916. Lost in Atlantic on a voyage from Gibraltar in 1922. Owner, A.E. Hickman.
Attainment:	380-ton tern built in New Brunswick in 1917. Lost in Cadiz Harbour, Spain, in 1919. Owner, W. Campbell.
Aureola:	288-ton barque built at Bidford, England, in 1873. Lost on a voyage from Scotland to NL in 1912. Owner, Bishop & Son.
Avalon:	312-ton brig built in England in 1863. Lost in the St. John's Narrows on a voyage from Scotland in 1884. Owner, William Walsh.

Avalon:	160-ton brig built in Bonavista Bay, NL in 1876. Lost at Cape Ballard in 1887. Owner, A. Goodrich.
A.V. Conrad:	147-ton tern built in Lahave, NS in 1918. Lost in the Atlantic in 1921. Owner, A.E. Hickman.
Banshee:	120-ton schooner built in Prince Edward Island in 1857. Lost in the Atlantic in 1867. Owner, J. Bowring.
Banshee:	99-ton schooner built in England in 1904. Lost in the Atlantic on a voyage to Spain in 1926. Owner, J. Bowring.
Barbara Barr:	229-ton brig built at Britannia Cove, Trinity Bay NL in 1918. Lost at Colinet Island on a voyage from Brazil in 1921. Owner, G.M. Barr
Bastian:	110-ton tern built in Denmark in 1920. Lost at Canso on a voyage to the West Indies in 1941. Owner, Moulton of Burin.
Beatrice:	99-ton brig built in England in 1901. Lost in the Atlantic on a voyage from Cadiz in 1911. Owner, Rorke of Carbonear.
Beatrice Vivian:	90-ton schooner built in Burin, NL in 1935. Lost at Cape Ray, NL in 1935. Owner, Hollett of Burin.

Bell of Burgeo:	Tern built in France in 1893. Lost on Sambro Ledge in 1918. Owner, J. Moulton.
Bella Rosa:	164-ton barque built in Brixham in 1874. Lost in the Atlantic on a voyage from Oporto in 1912. Owner, C. Bennett.
Benjamin Black:	128-ton brigantine built in England in 1832. Lost at St. Pierre in 1843. Owner, J.B. Barnes.
Benjamin. F. Phillips:	105-ton schooner built in Marystown NL. Lost in the Atlantic on a voyage from Oporto in 1912. Owner, P.E. Lake.
Bernard B. Conrad:	95-ton schooner built in NS. Lost in Atlantic on a voyage to Gibraltar in 1920.
Beothic:	141-ton brig built in Witless Bay, NL in 1828. Lost in the Atlantic in 1835. Registered at St. John's.
Bessie:	105-ton schooner built at Hr. Grace, NL in 1882. Lost on a voyage from Trepassey to Boston in 1887. Owner, Monroe.
Bessie:	61-ton schooner built at Moose River NS in 1870. Lost in the Atlantic in 1892. Owner, J. Munks.

SS *Beverley:* 1,013-ton steamship built at Baltimore, USA in 1885. Lost on a voyage to Gibraltar in 1920. Owner, G.C. Fearn.

Bianca: 313-ton tern built in Liverpool, NS in 1917. Lost on a voyage to Gibraltar in 1919. Owner, Bowrings.

Bismark: 110-ton schooner built in Maine in 1866. Lost on the Wadams, NL July 25, 1880 on a voyage to Gibraltar. Owner, Edward Duder.

Blanch: 270-ton barque built in Shelburne, NS in 1892. Lost on a voyage to Brazil in 1905. Owner, Job's.

Blanch: 313-ton barque built in Liverpool, NS, in 1911. Lost in the Atlantic in 1919. Owner, Bowrings.

Blanch: 78-ton schooner built in Yarmouth, NS in 1812. Lost in the Atlantic in 1825. Owner, N. Hoyles.

Blanch: 95-ton schooner built in Seal Cove in 1886. Lost in the Atlantic in 1905. Owner, J. Stewart.

Blue Jacket: 87-ton schooner built in Essex, NS in 1885. Lost on a voyage to Oporto in 1912.

Bluenose:	166-ton tern built in Falmouth, NS in 1903. Lost off Spain in 1919. Owner, A.E. Hickman.
Bohemia:	75-ton schooner built in Shelburne NS in 1903. Lost in ice off Cape Breton in 1927. Owner, Hollet of Burin.
Burleigh:	121-ton tern built in Shelburne, NS in 1904. Lost in the Atlantic on a voyage to Lisbon in 1919.
Callidora:	144-ton barque built in Port Madoc, Wales in 1901. Burnt in Carbonear Harbour in 1916. Owner, Rorke.
Camellia:	180-ton barque built in Devon, England in 1873. Lost at Scatarie, NS in 1891. Owner, L. Tessier.
Cape Bonavista:	138-ton auxiliary vessel built in Mahone Bay, NS in 1920. Lost off the NL Coast in 1946. Owner, F. Pine.
Cape Race:	332-ton tern built in Liverpool, NS in 1918. Lost at St. Shott's in 1932. Owner, R.G. Benson.
Caribou Hill:	99-ton schooner built in Essex MA, USA. Lost returning from Patras in 1919. Owner, McRae.
Carl R. Tibbo:	175-ton tern built in Grand Bank in 1919. Lost at Seldom-Come-By NL

	on a return voyage from Spain in 1919. Owner, Tibbo.
Carolin:	75-ton schooner built in PEI in 1885. Lost in mid-Atlantic in 1897. Owner, S. Knight.
Carolyn Schenk:	220-ton brig built in England in 1854. Lost at Petty Harbour Motion in 1860. Owner, Hounsel & Company.
Carranza:	95-ton schooner sank off Scatarie, NS in 1930 after being struck by lightening. Owned by Pushthrough firm.
Castle Carey:	80-ton schooner built at Grand Bank, NL in 1911. Lost in Atlantic on a voyage from Portugal in 1922. Owner, S. Harris.
Catherine M Moulton:	150-ton tern built at Lahave, NS in 1919. Lost on voyage to Oporto in 1925. Owner, R. Moulton.
Cecil Fern:	110-ton schooner built in Placentia in 1915. Lost off Spain in 1919. Owner, Fern.
Cecil Jr.:	204-ton tern built in Shelburne, NS in 1914. Lost on a return voyage from Seville in latitude 41.04 north, longitude 37.40 west in 1926. Owner, Capt. A. Kean.

C. Broyant:	141-ton tern built at Port Union, NL in 1928. Lost near Bermuda in 1928. Owner, Ellis.
Cecil L. Shave:	75-ton schooner built in Shelburne, NS in 1914. Lost on a voyage to Gibraltar in 1918. Owner T. Shave.
Celio:	140-ton barque built in England in 1895. Lost on a return voyage from Valencia in 1895. Owner, Rorke.
Cento:	90-ton schooner built in Lahave, NS in 1912. Lost on a voyage from Malaga in 1921. Owner, Templeton.
Ceres:	98-ton schooner built in the Bay of Islands, NL in 1834. Lost on a return voyage from Cadiz, Spain at Big Barachois, SMB, NL in 1838. Owner, L. Tessier.
Champion:	82-ton topsail schooner, built in Morton's Harbour, NL in 1885. Lost in the Atlantic. Owner, Monroe.
Charlotte Young:	302-ton barque built in England in 1867. Lost on a voyage to Pernambuco in 1880. Owner, Job.
Chautauqu:	354-ton tern built in Luneburg, NS, in 1918. Lost in mid-Atlantic in 1926. Owner, Monroe.

Checkers:	100-ton schooner built in NS. Lost on a voyage to Oporto in 1913. Owner, Crosbie.
Chedabucto:	185-ton brig built in NS in 1852. Lost in mid-Atlantic in 1870. Owner, Steward.
Chester Raymond:	79-ton tern built in Shelburne, NS in 1913. Lost off Portugal in 1919. Owner, S. Harris.
Christie & Eleanor:	143-ton schooner built in Shelburne, NS in 1922. Lost on a voyage to Gloucester in 1946. Owner, W. Forsey.
Clara:	145-ton brig built in Harbour Grace, NL in 1864. Lost in the Atlantic on a voyage to Lisbon in 1872. Owner, W. Donnelly.
Clara:	100-ton schooner built in Mahone Bay, NS in 1900. Lost on a voyage from the Mediterranean in 1912. Owner, McRay.
Clintonia:	99-ton schooner built in Gloucester. Destroyed by fire in mid-Atlantic in 1923. Owner, J. McRae.
Clutha:	224-ton barque built in Scotland in 1881. Lost in the ice south of Cape Race on a voyage to Brazil in 1923. Owner, Crosbie.

Confederation:	171-ton brig, lost in the Atlantic on a voyage from Oporto in 1895. Owner, Munn.
Corisande:	Barque, built in Devonshire in 1873. Lost near Cape Race on a return voyage from Brazil in 1899. Owner, Baine Johnson.
Corsair:	113-ton brig built in Hant's Harbour, Trinity Bay, NL in 1863. Lost at Cuckold's Cove on a return voyage from Europe.
Coronation:	98-ton schooner built in Shelburne, NS in 1903. Lost off Lisbon on a voyage to Cadiz in 1912. Owner, W. Tibbo.
Corona:	179-ton tern built in PEI in 1904. Lost off Cape Spear on a voyage from Barbados in 1912. Owner, R. Moulton.
Cote Nord:	147-ton tern built in Mahone Bay, NS in 1920. Lost on Petty Harbour Head in 1932. Owner, A. Genge.
County of Richmount:	245-ton tern built in Johnstown, Cape Breton, in 1919. Lost off Ramea in 1925. Owner, A Moulton.
Crafton McLeod:	85-ton schooner lost at Cappahayden, NL on a return voyage from Barbados in 1926. Ship owned in Spaniard's Bay.

Cyril T.:	117-ton tern built at River John, NS in 1918. Lost on Bear Cove Point on a return voyage from Maine in 1925.
Czarina:	299-ton barque built in Gosport, England in 1877. Lost in the Atlantic on a voyage to Pernambuco in 1924. Owner, Monroe.
Dahlia:	127-ton brig built in Devon in 1873. Lost in latitude 21.06 North longitude 62.10 west. Owner, L. Lester
Damaraland:	198-ton tern built in Liverpool in 1902. Lost in the Carribean in 1923. Owner, Goodridge.
David G. Ritchey:	284-ton tern built in Liverpool, NS in 1913. Lost in mid-Atlantic in 1924. Owner, G. Barr.
Dazzle:	100-ton tern built in Mahone Bay, NS in 1918. Lost off Ramea, NL on a voyage to Lisbon in 1940. Owner, A. Wareham.
Devonia:	270-ton barque built at Salem in 1886. Lost on a voyage to Brazil in 1912. Owner, Goodridge.
Dictator:	99-ton schooner built in Essex, NS in 1900. Sunk by enemy U-boat on a voyage to Oporto in 1918. Owner, H. Patten.

D. J. Thornhill:	Auxiliary vessel built in Grand Bank, NL. Lost in the Gulf of St. Lawrence on a voyage to New York in 1943. Owner, J. Thornhill.
Dolphin:	148-ton schooner built in PEI in 1843. Lost south of St. Pierre in 1843. Owner, Wight & Raddel.
Donald Hollett:	136-ton schooner built in Shelburne, NS in 1911. Lost the Atlantic in 1918. Owner, T. Hollett
Donald T.:	162-ton tern built in Shelburne, NS in 1920. Lost on a voyage to Gibraltar in 1921.
Dora:	205-ton brigantine built in England in 1866. Lost at Petty Harbour Head in 1875. Owner, Job Brothers.
Dorothy:	122-ton tern built in Wales in 1891. Sunk after a collision in the Straits of Gibraltar in 1905. Owner, J. Greaves.
Dorothy Baird:	a tern built in Portugal in 1920. Lost on a voyage from Pernambuco in latidude 24.42 north, longitude 53.07 west in 1930. Owner, J.S. Baird.
Dorothy Baird:	210-ton tern built at Liverpool, NS in 1907. Condemned at Baha, when she fell over in Dry dock in 1934. Owner. J. S. Baird.

Dorothy Dover:	63-ton school built in Green's Harbour. NL in 1916. Lost in the Atlantic in 1927.
Dorothy Duff:	152-ton tern built at Falmouth, NS in 1906. Sunk by enemy U-boat on voyage to Gibraltar in 1917. Owner, W. Duff.
Dorothy Lake:	238-ton tern built in Fortune, NL in 1911. Lost in the Atlantic in 1923. Owner, J. Lake.
Dorothy Louise:	125-ton tern built in Allendale, NS in 1910. Lost on a return voyage from Oporto in 1911. Owner, Harris.
Dolphin:	64-ton schooner built in Green Bay, NL. Lost in the Atlantic. Owner, H.T. Bartlett.
Douglas Haig:	99-ton schooner built in Monroe, Trinity Bay, NL. Lost through U-boat action on a voyage from Alicante in 1917. Owner, H. Stone.
Earl Kitchener:	Tern built in England. Lost on voyage to Oporto in 1916. Owner, Barr.
E.D. Bailey:	165-ton tern built in Louisburg, NS in 1918. Lost on a voyage to Brazil in 1924. Owner, Moores.
Edith Dawson:	397-ton tern built in Bridgewater, NS in 1918. Lost in mid-Atlantic in 1932. Owner, J. Penny.

Edith Legge:	233-ton tern built in Mahone Bay, NS in 1919. Lost in mid-Atlantic in 1929. Owner, J. Moulton.
Eileen Lake:	164-ton tern built in Fortune, NL in 1919. Lost on St. Pierre Banks, while on a voyage to Brazil.
Electra:	165-ton tern built in England in 1854. Lost on a voyage from Oporto in 1909. Owner, Goodridge.
Elfreda May:	90-ton schooner built Shelburne, NS in 1908. Lost on a voyage from Boston to St. John's in 1910. Owner, W. Patten.
Elin & Mary:	29-ton tern built in Essex, NS in 1912. Lost in St. Lawrence River in 1942. Owner, S. Tibbo.
Eliza Grieve:	149-ton brigantine built in England in 1854. Lost in the Atlantic on a voyage from Europe in 1862.
Elizabeth:	134-ton brigantine built in Carbonear, NL. Lost off Cape Race in 1875. Owner, Rorke.
Elizabeth Fern:	296-ton tern built in Placentia in 1917. Lost on a voyage to Alicante in 1920. Owner, Campbell & McKay.
Elizabeth Jane:	131-ton barque built in PEI in 1856. Lost in mid-Atlantic in 1884. Owner, Goodridge.

Elly:	254-ton auxiliary tern built in the Netherlands in 1918. Lost off Cape St. Mary's in 1926. Owner, Port Union Shipping.
Elsie:	90-ton schooner built in Sussex, NB in 1910. Lost off St. Pierre on a voyage to Gloucester in 1935. Owner, L. Kearley.
Elsie Corkum:	99-ton schooner built in Luneburg. NS Lost on voyage to Alicante in 1920. Owner, La Poile Export Company.
Elsie Burdette:	99-ton schoonr built in Mahone Bay, NS in 1914. Sunk by enemy U-boat on a voyage to Oporto in 1918. Owner, Job Brothers.
Emily Patten:	152-ton tern built in Shelburne, NS in 1916. Lost on a voyage from Turk's Island in 1929. Owner, J.B. Patten.
Emma:	280-ton brig built in England. Lost at Flat Rock in 1885.
Emma Belliveau:	152-ton tern built in NS in 1916. Lost on a return voyage from Setuba in 1926. Owner, F. Ellis
Emulator:	161-ton topsail schooner built in Scotland in 1878. Lost at Ferryland in 1902. Owner, Bennett.

Ena A. Moulton:	180-ton tern built in NS in 1919. Lost on a return voyage from Oporto in 1927. Owner, Moulton.
Enid E. Legge:	233-ton tern built in Mahone Bay. NS in 1919. Lost on a voyage home from Brazil in 1929. Owner, Moulton.
E.S. Hocken:	250-ton brigantine built in NS. Lost on a voyage from Cadiz in 1917. Owner, A.S. Randell.
Ester Hankinson:	292-ton tern built in Beeivau Cove in 1917. Lost in a mid-Atlantic voyage in 1924. Owner, G. Barr.
Ethel M. Bartlett:	92-ton schooner built in Shelburne, NS in 1914. Lost on a return voyage from Oporto in 1934. Owner, G. Bartlett of Burin.
Eva C.:	259-ton tern built in NS in 1909. lost in the Atlantic in 1918.
Evelyn:	287-ton tern built in Granville, NS in 1907. Lost on a voyage to Pernambuco in 1924. Owner, Job's.
Evelyn:	167-ton tern built in Shelburne, NS in 1899. Lost at Ferryland on a return voyage from Brazil in 1913. Owner, Crosbie.
Farling:	410-ton tern built in Weymouth in 1918. Lost on a voyage from Barbados in 1921. Owner, Job's.

Faustina:	146-ton tern built in Liverpool, NS in 1919. Lost on a voyage from Cadiz in 1930. Owner, Penney.
Fisherman:	130-ton tern built in Catalina in 1917. Sunk by enemy U-boat off the coast of Portugal in 1918. Owner, Fisherman's Protective Union.
Fleetwing:	233-ton barque built in Hall's Bay, NL in 1857. Condemned at Lisbon in 1873. Owner, J. Munn.
Flirtation:	83-ton schooner built in Essex, NS in 1901. Sunk by enemy U-boat off the coast of Spain in 1917. Owner, A. Beck.
Flora M. Sperry:	106-ton schooner built at Lahave, NS in 1892. Lost off Scatarie NS in 1907. Owner, Ryan.
Florence Swyer:	157-ton tern built at Charlottown, NL in 1918. Lost off the Spanish Coast in 1925. Owner, A.E. Hickman.
Flowermen:	306-ton tern built in Shelburne. NS in 1918. Lost on a voyage from Turks Island in 1927. Owner, J. Patten.
Francis:	259-ton tern built in Waymouth, NS in 1903. Lost at Calais France in 1914. Owner, J. S. Baird.
Freedom:	197-ton tern built in Liverpool, NS in 1906. Lost on a voyage from St.

John's to Sydney in 1924. Owner, A.S. Randell.

Francis E. Moulton: 208-ton tern built in Mahone Bay, NS in 1919. Lost at Cape Ray in 1925. Owner, J.T. Moulton.

Frank Baxter: 142-ton schooner built in Lahave NS in 1919. Lost on a voyage home from Cadiz in 1932. Owner, A. Wareham.

Galatea: 138-ton barque built in Weymouth, England in 1884. Lost on a return voyage from Santa Pola in 1915. Owner, J. S. Baird.

Gaspe: Topsail barque, built in Liverpool, NS. Lost off Barbados in 1922.

G.A. Wood: 120-ton schooner built in NS. Lost coming from Barbados in 1929. Owner, Duff.

Gay Gordon: 119-ton tern built in NS in 1907. Lost in ice on a voyage home from Oporto in 1919. Owner, Harvey & Co.

G. Blanche: 280-ton tern built in Liverpool, NS. Lost on the coast of Brazil in 1919. Owner, J. Williams.

General Allenby: 155-ton tern built in Grand Bank, NL in 1919. Lost on a voyage from Barbados in 1930. Owner, S. Harris.

General Byng: 169-ton tern built in Marystown, NL in 1918. Lost in the Atlantic on a voyage from Turk's Island in 1928. Owner, P.L. Carr.

General Currie: 162-ton tern built in Grand Bank, NL in 1918. Lost off Miquelon in 1922. Owner, S. Harris.

General Gough: 198-ton tern built in Essex, NS in 1920. Lost on a return voyage from Lisbon in 1935. Owner, C. Harris.

General Horn: 178-ton tern built in Shelburne, NS in 1919. Lost in the Atlantic on a return voyage from Cadiz in 1927.

General Knox: 145-ton tern built in Marystown, NL in 1919. Lost in mid-Atlantic in 1919. Owner, C. Harris.

General Laurie: 198-ton tern built in Allendale, NS in 1908. Lost through U-boat action in 1917. Owner, Barr.

General Plumber: 149-ton tern built in Allendale, NS in 1919. Lost on a return voyage from Barbados in 1930.

General Rawinson: 149-ton tern built at Marystown, NL in 1920. Condemned at Oporto in 1922. Owner, Marystown Trading company.

General Smuts: 159-ton tern built at Shelburne, NS in 1918. Lost in mid-Atlantic in 1926. Owner, G. Harris.

General Trenchard:	149-ton tern built in Allendale, NS in 1920. Lost in the Atlantic on a voyage from Oporto in 1929.
Geisha:	130-ton tern built in Appledore, NS in 1906. Lost off Cape Spear on a return voyage from Cadiz in 1906. Owner, R. Cook.
George B. Cluett:	182-ton auxiliary vessel built at Lahave, NS in 1920. Lost off Cape North in 1941.
George Ewart:	148-ton tern built in Fortune, NL in 1913. Sunk in a collision off Gibraltar in 1917. Owner, J.E. Lake.
Gladys Fearn:	100-ton tern built in Lahave, NS in 1912. Lost in the Atlantic in 1919. Owner, G. Fearn.
Gladys J. Hollett:	150-ton tern built in Shelburne, NS in 1917, Lost off Cape Race in 1923. Owner, Hollett.
Gladys Street:	123-ton tern built in NS in 1919. Lost in the Atlantic in 1920.
Glengarry:	160-ton brig built in Weymouth, England in 1884. Lost on a return voyage from Santa Pola in 1915. Owner, J. S. Baird.
Golden Bell:	79-ton schooner built in Mahone Bay, NS in 1908. Lost on a voyage to Gibraltar in 1926. Owner, J. Petite.

Golden Hind: 188-ton tern built in Liverpool, NS in 1893. Lost on a return voyage from Pernambuco in 1911. Owner, R. Bishop.

Gordon C. Fudge: 150-ton tern built in Essex, MA in 1917. Lost on a return voyage from Gibraltar in 1922. Owner, E. Fudge.

Gordon E. Moulton: 195-ton tern built at Day Spring in 1919. Lost off Burgeo in 1924. Owner, J. Moulton.

Gordon T. Tibbo: 194-ton tern built in NS in 1918. Lost in Mid-Atlantic in 1926. Owner, G.C Ballem.

Governor Harvey: 135-ton brigantine built in PEI in 1831. Lost at sea in 1847. Owner, C.F. Bennett.

Grace: 139-ton topsail schooner built in England in 1883. Lost on a return voyage from Cadiz in 1912. Owner, Goodridge.

Grace: 96-ton tern built at Port Madoc, Wales in 1907. Lost at sea in 1917. Owner, A. Garland.

Grand Falls: 145-ton tern built in Shelburne, NS in 1910. Lost in mid-Atlantic in 1914.

Gratis: 157-ton barque built in Scilly in 1879. Lost on a return voyage from Oporto in 1908. Owner, A. Goodridge.

Gwendolen Warren:	274-ton tern built at Liverpool, NS in 1916. Lost in ice off St. John's. Owner, Bowrings.
Gwladys:	150-ton schooner built at Wales in 1892. Lost on a voyage to Bristol in 1908. Owner, W. Duff.
Harlet:	141-ton tern built in Trinity Bay, NL in 1921. Lost in the Argentia area in 1921. Owner Monroe.
Harmony:	Brig built in New Perlican, NL in 1877. Lost on a voyage to Barbados in 1931. Owner, J. Munn.
Harp:	147-ton brigantine built in PEI in 1865. Lost on voyage to Cadiz in 1874. Owner, H. Hayward.
Harriet:	Barque built in Dorset in 1873. Lost at Pouch Cove in 1882. Owner, Bowrings.
Harriet:	80-ton schooner built in Denmark in 1910. Lost on a voyage to Oporto in 1925. Owner, Crosbie.
Harry & Verna:	257-ton tern built in Essex, NS in 1919. Lost on a voyage to Barbados in 1931. Owner, J.S. Baird.
Hawanee:	Vessel built in Lunenburg, NS in 1909. Sunk on a voyage from Cadiz by enemy U-boat in 1918. Owner, Tessier.

Hazel Trahey:	145-ton tern built in Parrsboro, NS in 1910. Lost in the Atlantic on a voyage from Cadiz in 1926. Owner, W. Grieve.
Heather:	150-ton brig built at Malignant Cove in 1854. Lost south of Cape Spear in 1856. Owner, J. Grieve.
Helen Isobel:	167-ton barque built in Greennock in 1867. Lost on a voyage from Barbados in 1904. Owner, Baine Johnston.
Helen Jean:	129-ton tern built in Milltown, NL in 1920. Lost in the Caribbean.
Helen Stewart:	180-ton tern built in Lunenburg, NS in 1893. Lost at Cape Race on a voyage from Barbados in 1904. Owner, A.E. Hickman.
Herbert Fern:	325-ton tern built in Placentia, NL in 1919. Lost in mid-Atlantic in 1919.
Herbert L. Rawdihi:	1,190-ton, four-masted vessel, built in MA, USA in 1919. Lost off Cape St. Vincent on a voyage to Cadiz in 1947. Owner, Wareham.
Herbert & Ruby:	98-ton schooner built at Marystown, NL. Lost on a voyage to Portugal in 1917. Owner, Hollett.
Herbert Warren:	272-ton tern built at Gross Cocque in 1917. Lost in the mid-Atlantic in 1919. Owner, Warren.

Hester Hankinson:	292-ton tern built in Essex. MA in 1917. Lost on a voyage from Cadiz in 1924.
Hilda R.:	99-ton tern built in Lahave, NS in 1910. Sunk off Spain by enemy U-boat in 1917. Owner, A.S. McRea.
Hiram H:	359-ton tern built in NS. Lost at Bell Island, C.B., NL in 1924. Owner, A.S. Randell.
Hiram MacLean:	447-ton tern built at Economy, NS in 1919. Lost off Norfolk Virginia in 1919. Owner, Penny & Co.
Hope:	98-ton schooner built at Carbonear, NL. Lost in the Atlantic in 1856. Owner, Rorke.
Howard Primrose:	91-ton schooner built in Chance Harbour in 1849. Lost at sea in 1856. Owner, J. Hogsett.
Huntley:	141-ton tern built in Scott's Bay, NS in 1919. Lost at Motion Head on a return voyage from Turks Island in 1921. Owner, Tessier.
Ich Dien:	Barque built at Avon, NS in 1900. Lost by fire in St. John's Harbour in 1908. Owner, Crosbie.
Ida D. Bishop:	93-ton schooner built in Shelburne, NS. Sunk in the Atlantic by enemy U-boat in 1918. Owner, R.K. Bishop.

Idalia: 98-ton schooner built in Bay Roberts, NL in 1889. Lost on a return voyage from Portugal in 1916. Owner, A. Dawe.

Impramus: 177-ton tern built at Port Blandford, NL in 1917. Lost south of Bermuda in 1921. Owner, A.E. Hickman.

Independence: 145-ton tern built in NS. Lost on voyage from Santa Pola in 1916. Owner, Hiscock.

Inspiration: 283-ton tern built in NS in 1917. Owner, J. S. Baird.

Isabella: 140-ton brig built in England in 1873. Lost on a return voyage from Brazil at St. Mary's Bay in 1881. Owner, Job.

Isabella: 148-ton brig built in Liverpool, NS in 1904. Lost at Cape St. Francis in 1860 on a return voyage from England. Owner, J. Bowring.

Isabel Moore: 157-ton tern built in Liverpool, NS in 1920. Lost in Fortune Bay in 1930. Owner, F. Pine.

Ivanhoe: 99-ton schooner built at Liverpool, NS in 1904. Lost on a voyage to the Bahamas in 1916. Owner, Moulton.

James Burton Coor: 98-ton schooner built in Lunenburg, NS in 1913. Sunk by enemy U-boat off Gibraltar in 1916. Owner, Smith & Company.

James O'Neil: 98-ton topsail schooner built in Ireland in 1905. Lost in ice off Cape Race on a return voyage from Spain in 1943.

James & Stanley: 111-ton auxiliary vessel built in Shelburne, NS in 1918. Lost on a voyage from Boston. Owner G. Handrigan.

James Stewart: 97-ton brig built in Indian Arm in 1877. Lost in the Atlantic in 1884. Owner, J. Syme.

J.B. Kitchener: 300-ton brig built in NS. Lost on a voyage to Queenstown in 1919. Owner, Moulton.

Jean: Tern built in Liverpool, NS in 1905. Sunk by German raider while on a return voyage from Brazil in 1916. Owner, Crosbie.

Jean D. Duff: 345-ton tern built in Mahone Bay, NS 1917. Lost on a voyage from Scotland in 1923. Owner, Baine Johnston.

Jean & Mary: 194-ton tern built in Marystown, NL in 1918. Lost on the Penguin Islands NL in 1921. Owner, A. Buffett.

Jean McKay:	194-ton tern built in Marystown, NL in 1918. Lost on a voyage from Oporto in 1930. Owner, F. Stoodley.
Jean Smith:	108-ton schooner built in Belleoram, NL in 1920, Lost off Cape St. George on a voyage to Gloucester in 1934. Owner, A. Kearley.
J.E. Conrad:	95-ton schooner built in NS. Lost off Fayal in 1941. Owner, J.B. Petten.
Jennie E. Richey:	97-ton schooner built Shelburne NS, in 1910. Lost at Patras on a voyage to Sicily in 1919. Owner, A.E. Hickman.
Jenny Duff:	110-ton schooner built in Bridgewater, NS in 1911. Lost on a voyage from Lisbon in 1917. Owner, L.B. Clark.
Jessie:	80-ton schooner built in Morton's Harbour, NL in 1886. Lost in the Atlantic in 1907. Owner, E.J. Duder.
Jessie L. Smith:	120-ton schooner lost in mid-Atlantic in 1909. Owner, Crosbie.
Jessey:	93-ton schooner built in NS in 1857. Lost in mid-Atlantic in 1890. Owner, S. Randell.
Jessy:	117-ton brig built in Lunenburg, NS in 1901. Lost at Burnt Island on a voyage from Barbados in 1934. Owner, Job.

Joan Hickman:	295-ton tern built at Charlottown, NL in 1917. Lost on the Spanish Coast in 1920. Owner, A.E. Hickman.
John:	299-ton barque, built in Wellington in 1875. Lost on a return voyage from Cadiz in 1919. Owner, W. Grieve.
John E. Lake:	202-ton tern built in Fortune, NL in 1919. Lost on the Brazilian Coast in 1920. Owner, J. Lake.
John Harvey:	100-ton tern built in Belleoram, NL in 1909. Lost At Gabarous, NS in 1912. Owner, G. Kearley.
J. Miller:	353-ton tern built in Noel, NS in 1918. Lost in the Mediterranean in 1921. Owner, J. Petite.
John Millett:	167-ton tern built in Shelburne, NS in 1919. Lost on a return voyage from Oporto in 1933. Owner, G. Harris.
J. N. Rufus:	212-ton tern built in Lahave, NS in 1913. Lost on a voyage from Oporto in 1922.
J.R. Gardner:	Schooner built in Liverpool, NS in 1916. Lost in mid-Atlantic in 1919. Owner, Bowrings.
John W. Miller:	266-ton tern built in Mahone Bay, NS in 1918. Lost on a voyage to Brazil in 1931. Owner, Crosbie.

Jost:	234-ton brig built in Port Grenville, NS in 1910. Lost in mid-Atlantic in 1918. Owner, Randell.
Julia:	144-ton brigantine built in Bristol in 1874. Lost in the Narrows at start of voyage to the Mediterranean in 1876. Owner, G.A. Hayward.
June:	480-ton tern built in Oregon, USA in 1875. Lost in the Mediterranean in 1922. Owner, Baine Johnston.
Jura:	234-ton brig built in Miramici, NB in 1863.. Lost in mid-Atlantic in 1875. Owner, Walters.
Kalmea:	172-ton brig built in England in 1872. Lost on a return voyage from Europe in 1890. Owner, L. Tessier.
Kate:	85-ton schooner built in Heart's Content, NL in 1874. Lost on voyage to Mediterranean in 1894. Owner, Rorke.
Kate Cummings:	184-ton brig built in North Sydney, NS in 1862. Lost at Cow Bay, NS in 1870. Owner, P. Cummings.
Kinsman:	350-ton tern built at Charlottetown, NL in 1919. Lost on voyage to Gibraltar in 1922. Owner, A.E. Hickman.

L. Borden:	99-ton St. John's schooner lost on a voyage from New York in 1935.
Lady May:	70-ton schooner built at Little Bras, Cape Breton in 1878. Lost at Torbay in 1897. Owner, J. Steer.
Lady Mulgrave:	108-ton schooner built at Arichat, NS in 1858. Lost in the Atlantic in 1875. Owner, T.N. Mallory.
Lady Napier:	210-ton brigantine built at Georgetown in 1902. Lost off Cape Race on a voyage to Brazil in 1911. Owner, Crosbie.
Lady Thorburn:	64-ton schooner built in British Harbour, NL in 1889. Lost at Cape Breton in 1924. Owner, A. Gardiner.
Lake Simcoe:	337-ton barque built in Scotland in 1871. Lost in the Atlantic in 1915. Owner, Baine Johnston.
Lawrence A. Moulton:	248-ton tern built in Northumberland Strait, NS in 1918. Lost by fire at Sydney NS in 1920. Owner, J.T. Moulton.
Lavinia:	125-ton schooner built in Lunenburg, NS in 1846. Lost at Pouch Cove on a voyage to the Meditereanean in 1876. Owner, J. McGregor.

Lavonia:	98-ton schooner built at Cowes, England in 1871. Lost on voyage to Pernambuco in 1907. Owner, Duff.
Lawson:	274-ton tern built at Port Greville, NS in 1909. Lost in the Atlantic in 1919. Owner, W. Grieve.
Little Stephano:	125-ton tern built at Shelburne, NS in 1917. Lost in mid-Atlantic in 1926. Owner. Capt. A. Kean.
Little Princess:	199-ton tern built in Lahave, NS in 1919. Lost in mid-Atlantic in 1923. Owner, Capt. A. Kean.
Little Secret:	98-ton schooner built at Marystown, NL. Lost on voyage to South America in 1917.
Lila A. Boutelier:	96-ton schooner built at Essex, MA, USA in 1901. Lost on Voyage to Oporto in 1912. Owner, C. Steer.
Lila E.D. Young:	155-ton tern built at Louisburg, NS in 1919. Lost off the Spanish coast in 1930. Owner, Moulton.
Lima:	160-ton brig built in England. Lost at Petty Harbour Motion in 1853. Owner, Job Brothers.
Lizzie:	149-ton schooner built at Heart's Content, NL. Lost on a voyage to Lisbon in 1881. Owner, J & W. Boyd.

Lizzie:	81-ton schooner built in Trinity Bay in 1867. Lost in the Atlantic in 1890. Owner, W. Butt.
Lizzie:	113-ton brigantine built in Heart's Content, NL in 1879. Lost in the Atlantic in 1881. Owner, Rorke.
Lolita:	176-ton tern built in Liverpool, NS in 1913. Lost in the Atlantic. Owner, C & A Dawe.
Lolita A:	179-ton tern built in Liverpool, NS in 1908. Lost in mid-Atlantic in 1917.
Lottie A. Silver:	Schooner, lost through a collision near Gibraltar in 1917. Owner, Forward & Tibbo.
Louise:	164-ton steam ship built in Paisley, Scotland in 1892. Lost at sea in 1910. Owner, Crosbie.
Louise Hickman:	Tern built in NS. Lost on a return voyage from Portugal in 1921. Owner, A.E. Hickman.
Lucey House:	98-ton schooner built in Grand Bank, NL in 1911. Sunk by enemy U-boat off Gibraltar in 1917. Owner, J. Smith. Hr. Breton, crew landed at Gibraltar.
Lucille:	164-ton tern built at Parrisboro in 1906. Lost on voyage to Pernambuco in 1907. Owner, Crosbie.

Ludwig:	130-ton tern built in Denmark in 1918. Lost at Malaga, Spain in 1921. Owner, Randell & Company.
Lutzen:	278-ton motor vessel built Fort William, NL in 1918. Lost off Cape Cod in 1939. Owner, Job Brothers.
Mable Davis:	188-ton tern built in Boyd's Arm, NL in 1918. Lost in Atlantic in 1919. Owner, W. Davis.
Mable F. Frye:	1,153-ton four-masted vessel built in MA. Lost in mid-Atlantic in 1936. Owner, Rodway.
Maggie:	178-ton barque built in Troon, Scotland in 1883. Lost on a voyage from Oporto in 1912. Owner, J.S. Baird.
Maggie E.:	100-ton schooner built in Fortune, NL. Lost on the South Coast in 1926. Owned by Patten.
Majorie Mahaffey:	143-ton tern built in Mahone Bay, NS in 1918. Lost at Mistaken Point in 1921. Owner, Randell.
Maple Leaf:	196-ton tern built at Chester Basin, NS in 1901. Lost on voyage to Europe. Owner, Smith.
Margaret Moulton:	174-ton tern built at Dayspring, NS in 1918. Lost in the Atlantic in 1919. Owner, J. Moulton.

Marguerite Ryan: 147-ton tern built in Shelburne, NS in 1920. Lost on a voyage from Bahia in 1914. Owner, W.R. Howley.

Marie Louise: 400-ton tern built at Charlottetown, NL in 1919. Lost on a return voyage from Spain in 1920.

Marinee: Barque built in England in 1874. Lost on a voyage from Portugal in 1884. Owner, Goodridge.

Marion Mosher: 84-ton schooner built at Lunenburg, NS in 1910. Lost off Miquelon in 1948.

Marjorie McGlachin: 180-ton tern built in Liverpool, NS in 1915. Lost in Portugal in 1918. Owner, A.E. Hickman.

Mark H. Gray: 100-ton schooner built in Fortune, NL . Lost on voyage from Oporto in 1933. Owned by Fortune firm.

Mary D. Young: 99-ton tern built in Lunenburg, NS in 1912. Lost off St. Pierre in 1918. Owner, S. Piercy.

Mary Hendry: 249-ton tern built in Liverpool, NS in 1899. Lost in the Burgeo area in 1916. Owner, Moulton.

Mauna Loa: 99-ton schooner, built in Lunenburg, NS in 1901. Lost after grounding at Gibraltar in 1917.

May:	110-ton schooner built in Trinity Bay. NL. Lost in mid-Atlantic in 1851. Owner, Howley.
May:	156-ton brig built in England in 1873. Lost on a voyage to England in 1889. Owner, R. Randell.
Mayflower:	138-ton schooner built in Pistolet Bay in 1879. Lost on voyage from Bahia in 1914. Owner, A. Goodridge.
Max Horton:	139-ton tern built in Lahave, NS in 1918. Lost in the Atlantic in 1926. Owner, Forsey.
McLure:	191-ton tern built in Tatamaogouche, NS in 1900. Sunk by enemy U-boat off the Spanish Coast in 1917. Owner, J.T. Moulton.
Menthol:	120-ton schooner built in Harbour Grace, NL in 1876. Lost on a voyage from Alicante in 1892. Owner, Munn
Meteor:	140-ton barque built in Exploits, NL in 1885. Lost on voyage to Cadiz in 1890. Owner, M. Munroe.
Mikado:	57-ton schooner built in Smith Sound, NL in 1887. Lost in the Atlantic in 1887. Owner, A.E. Hickman.

Mildred:	166-ton tern built in Lunenburg, NS in 1907. Lost on a voyage to Portugal in 1918. Owner, G. Barr.
Mildred Adams:	147-ton schooner built in Mahone Bay, NS in 1917. Lost off the Azores in 1932. Owner E. Collett.
Milnorian:	366-ton tern built in Port Greville, NS in 1918. Lost in the Atlantic in 1921. Owner, J. Moulton.
Minas Queen:	456-ton tern built in Parrsboro, NS in 1887. Sunk off French Coast by enemy U-boat in 1916. Owner, Job Brothers.
Mina Swim:	70-ton schooner built in Essex, NS in 1904. Lost in the Atlantic in 1917. Owner, Lefeuvre.
Minnie:	164-ton brigantine built in Bideford, England in 1875. Lost on voyage from Barbados at Cape Breton in 1887. Owner, A. Goodridge.
Mintie:	100-ton schooner built in Trinity Bay, NL in 1918. Lost on voyage to Oporto in 1921. Owner, W. Coaker.
Miriam:	358-ton tern built in NS in 1918. Lost at Wabana, Bell Island, NL in 1924.
Molega:	148-ton tern built in NS in 1881. Lost on a voyage to Figuera in 1917. Owner, A. Lawrence.

Mollie Fern: 120-ton tern built at Placentia, NL in 1920. Lost at Bonavista in 1950.

Monchey: 118-ton tern built in Harbour Grace, NL in 1919. Lost in the Atlantic in 1920. Owner, Tessier.

Moniter: 110-ton schooner built in Essex, NS in 1909. Sunk in the Mediterranean by enemy U-boat in 1917. Owner, P. Templeton.

Montrose: 198-ton tern built at Shelburn, NS in 1906. Lost at Peter's River, St. Mary's Bay, on a return voyage from Pernambuco in 1910. Owner, Job.

Motherland 11: 384-ton tern built at Annapolis, NS in 1917. Lost off Mauritus in 1922.

Myrtle Piercey: 198-ton tern built in Liverpool, NS in 1919. Lost on a voyage to Valencia in 1926. Owner, S. Piercey.

Mystery: 80-ton schooner built in Fortune, NL in 1892. Lost at St. Shott's on a voyage from Brazil in 1897. Owner, J. Kelley.

Mystery: 98-ton schooner built at Essex, MA, USA in 1898. Lost on voyage to Gibraltar in 1908. Owner, Duff.

Nancy Lee: 114-ton tern built in Campbellton, NL in 1920. Lost on voyage to Spain in 1925. Owner, Horwood.

Naomi: 126-ton brigantine built in Heart's Content, NL in 1857. Lost at Outer Cove in 1871. Owner, G. Ehlers.

Neerod: 129-ton tern built in Norris Arm, NL in 1919. Lost on Carbonear Island in 1919. Owner, G. Glenny.

Nellie F.Harris: Schooner built in Grand Bank, NL. Lost off Cape Breton in 1906. Owner, Harris.

Nellie Louise: 243-ton tern built at Lahave, NS in 1901. Lost on voyage from Barbados in 1916. Owner, Bowrings.

Nellie M: 231-ton barque built in Burnt Bay in 1900. Lost in mid-Atlantic. Owner, Moores.

Neptune 11: 100-ton schooner built in Denmark in 1929. Lost in mid-Atlantic in 1935. Owner, Forward & Tibbo.

Nerett: 60-ton schooner built at Salt Pond, Burin, NL in 1908. Lost in mid-Atlantic in 1919. Owner, Ryan.

Netherton: 133-ton brig built in Trinity Bay. NL Lost on Miquelon Island on a voyage from Turks Island in 1933. Owner, Besion.

Neva: 242-ton brig built in Bathurst, NB in 1863. Lost at Lisbon in 1875. Owner, L. Tessier.

Newton S. Lake: 151-ton tern built at Belleoram, NL in 1920. Lost off Portugal in 1921. Owner, Lake.

Nina Bouillier: Schooner lost on a voyage to Oporto in 1922. Owner, Steers.

Nina L.: 95-ton tern built in Notre Dame Bay, NL in 1906. Lost in the Atlantic in 1911. Owner, Crosbie.

Nina Lee: 97-ton schooner built in Allendale, NS in 1913. Lost on return voyage from Piraeus in 1921. Owner, J. Foote.

Nina L.C.: 355-ton tern built in Port Union, NL in 1918. Lost on return voyage from Brazil in 1918. Owner, Port Union Fisheries.

Nimrod: Schooner built in Harbour Main, NL in 1853. Lost in ice on a voyage to Barbados in 1897. Owner, J. Munn.

Nobility: 99-ton schooner built in Mahone Bay, NS in 1902. Lost on a voyage from Oporto in 1920. Owner, Piercy & Tibbo.

Nordica: 123-ton schooner built in Allendale, NS in 1912. Lost on voyage to Cadiz in 1921. Owner, Patten & Forsey.

Norman B. Strong: 157-ton tern built in Little Bay Islands, NL in 1918. Lost on a voyage to Corsica in 1922. Owner, W.S. Monroe.

Novelty: 266-ton tern built in Port Greville, NS in 1910. Lost on voyage to Pernambuco in 1926. Owner, Barr.

Octavae: Barquentine lost at Ferryland in 1886. Owner, Baine Johnston.

Olinda: 227-ton brigantine built in Liverpool, NS in 1899. Lost on the Labrador with a load of fish for Spain in 1919. Owner, Rorke.

Olinda: Barque built in Greennock, Scotland in 1839. Lost at Sable Island in 1886. Owner, Duder.

Olive Moore: 158-ton tern built in Liverpool, NS in 1920. Lost on voyage to Malaga in 1930. Owner, F. Pine.

Onato: Schooner built at Essex, MA, USA in 1905. Lost in the Atlantic in 1919. Owner, Inkpen.

Optimist: 110-ton tern built in Glovertown, NL in 1919. Lost on a voyage home from Oporto in 1922. Owner, A.E. Hickman.

Oregon: 110-ton schooner built by Smith & Rhuland. Lost in the Atlantic in 1918. Owner, Harris.

Orieron:	150-ton brig built in PEI in 1872. Lost on the Brazilian Coast in 1882. Owner, L. Tessier.
Over The Top:	166-ton tern built in Birchy Bay, NL in 1919, Lost on a voyage home from Brazil in 1928. Owner, Bishop.
Olwin:	154-ton schooner built at Pembroke in 1886. Lost on a return voyage from Torrevelia, Spain in 1922. Owner, Munn.
Parejero:	345-ton barque built in Greenock, Scotland in 1870. Lost on a voyage from Barbados at Petty Harbour in 1882. Owner, Baine Johnston.
Paragon:	Schooner built in Notre Dame Bay, NL in 1891. Lost on home voyage from Cadiz in 1922. Owner, Crosbie.
Pauline Martin:	298-ton tern built at Norris Arm, NL in 1917. Lost on a return voyage from Cadiz in 1919. Owner, M.E. Martin.
Pearl Eveline:	99-ton schooner built at Lunenburg, NS in 1900. Lost on voyage to Oporto in 1913. Owner, H. Smith.
Pearl Eveline:	Schooner built at Horton in 1881. Lost on a voyage to Oporto in 1929.

Pelleen:	389-ton tern built at Port Blandford, NL in 1919. Lost in the Atlantic in 1924. Owner, A. Williams.
Penguin:	180-ton brigantine built in England in 1856. Lost at Cape St. Francis on a voyage to Exeter in 1873. Owner, Munn.
Pere Marquette:	172-ton schooner built in Michigan in 1890. Lost on voyage to New York in 1917. Owner, H. Smith.
Piercy Roy:	110-ton schooner sunk by a U-boat on a voyage to Santa Pola in 1917. Owner, Smith.
Perceptor:	100-ton schooner built in Essex, NS in 1899. Lost off Nova Scotia in 1920. Owner, Buffett.
Peerless:	147-ton brig built in Greenock in 1859. Lost in the Atlantic on a voyage from the UK in 1865. Owner, R. Rhodes.
Percy Wells:	119-ton schooner built in Hare Bay, NL in 1919. Lost on return voyage from New York in 1921. Owner, Horwood.
Pearl:	163-ton schooner built in Horton in 1818. Lost off Cape Hatteras in 1894.

Phileen:	266-ton tern built at Dartmouth, NS in 1917. Lost in mid-Atlantic in 1919. Owner, A.S. Randell.
President Coaker:	260-ton tern built in Port Union, NL in 1919. Lost at Cape Race on a return voyage from Brazil in 1924. Owner, Fisherman's Protective Union.
Procyon:	89-ton schooner built in MA, USA in 1889. Lost on the Labrador in 1914. Owner, Munn.
Queenie B:	83-ton schooner built at Belleoram, NL in 1918. Lost on a return voyage from Oporto in 1920. Owner, Harris.
Ramah:	95-ton schooner built in the USA in 1905. Lost at Oporto in 1912. Owner, S. Harris.
Revenue:	118-ton schooner built at Lunenburg, NS in 1908. Lost in the Atlantic in 1919.
Red Gauntlet:	74-ton schooner built at Jersey, Channel Islands,1906. Lost on voyage from Cadiz in 1908.
Reliance:	120-ton schooner built in Lunenburg, NS in 1900. Lost off Cadiz in 1912.
Renown:	Schooner lost on a voyage home from Oporto in 1911. Owner, Moulton.

Retraction:	143-ton tern built in Lahave, NS in 1916. Lost in latitude 33.06 north, longitude 33.19 west on a voyage to Spain in 1926. Owner, P. Templeton.
Revenue:	118-ton schooner built in Lunenburg, NS in 1908. Lost in the Atlantic in 1918.
Ria:	154-ton tern built in Marystown, NL in 1920. Lost on a voyage from Cadiz. Owner, G. & A. Forsey.
Richard:	90-ton schooner built at Essex, MA, USA in 1907. Lost on voyage from Cadiz in 1917. Owner, Hollett.
Rickets V.C.:	155-ton tern built in Lahave, NS in 1919. Lost in the Carribean on voyage from Santo Domingo in 1921, Owner, Patten & Forsey.
Rita M. Cluett:	85-ton schooner built at Shellburn, NS in 1917. Lost on a voyage from Oporto in 1923. Owner, Harvey.
Robert J. Dale:	197-ton tern built in Liverpool, NS in 1914. Lost in St. Mary's Bay in 1924 on a voyage from Philadelphia. Owner, G. M. Barr.
Robert Max:	120-ton schooner built in Shelburne, NS in 1919. Sunk by U-boat on a voyage to Portugal in 1941. Owners G. B. Fisheries.

Robert Ray:	164-ton tern built in Grand Bank, NL in 1920. Crushed in ice in the Atlantic in 1921. Owners, S. Harris.
Roma:	115-ton schooner built in Shelburne, NS in 1899. Sunk by U-boat in Mediterranean on a voyage to Oporto in 1916. Owner, Baine Johnston.
Ronald B. Moulton:	138-ton tern built in Lahave, NS in 1918. Lost on a voyage to Oporto in 1921. Owner, Moulton.
Ronald M. Douglas:	149-ton tern built in Bay d'Espoir in 1919. Lost on a voyage to Cadiz in 1930. Owner, W. Garland.
Rose M.:	148-ton tern built in Norris Arm, NL in 1919. Lost at Fayal in 1922.
Rose Dorothea:	133-ton schooner built in Essex, NS in 1905. Sunk by U-boat on a return voyage from Spain in 1917.
Rose of Torridge:	Topsail Schooner built in Wales in 1895. Lost on a voyage from Cadiz in 1912. Owner, Munn.
Roy Bruce:	150-ton tern built in Shelburne, NS in 1920. Lost in a collision off Cape Race in 1924 on a voyage from Banaza. Owner, Hollett.
Ruby W.:	286-ton schooner built in Liverpool, NS in 1917. Lost on a voyage from

	Pernambuco in 1922. Owner, Baine Johnston.
Russel Lake:	125-ton tern built in Fortune, NL in 1919. Lost at Burgeo in 1929. Owner, J. Lake.
Ruth Hickman:	386-ton tern built in Charlottetown, NL in 1918. Lost off Ireland in 1920. Owner, A.E. Hickman.
Samuel Courtney:	441-ton tern built at Noel, NS in 1918. Lost at Gibraltar in 1920. Owner, G.M. Barr.
Saucy Arethusa:	144-ton tern built at Essex, NS in 1917. Lost on Sambro, Halifax in 1929. Owner, A. Ashburn.
Sea Mew:	113-ton brig built at PEI in 1854. Lost in mid-Atlantic in 1868. Owner, William McCarthy.
Searchlight:	146-ton tern built at Souris, PEI in 1901. Lost on a voyage from Oporto in 1905. Owner, Bowrings.
Selma Creaser:	124-ton tern built in Shelburne, NS in 1918. Lost on a voyage from Portugal in 1927. Owner, S. Cluett.
Senif:	327-ton steamship built in Ontario in 1918. Lost on Nova Scotia coast in 1855.

Shamrock:	134-ton brigantine built in Carbonear NL in 1885, Lost off Cape Harrison in 1901. Owner, Rorke.
Sidney Smith:	145-ton topsail schooner built in Wales in 1885. Lost on voyage to Gibraltar in 1917. Owner, Ashburn.
Silver Queen:	134-ton schooner built at Selmah in 1915. Lost off Spanish Coast in 1924. Owner, A. Lindsay.
Silver Sea:	Squared-rigged vessel built in England. Lost at St. Shott's on a voyage from Brazil. Owner, Bowerings.
Silver Spray:	A tern lost on a voyage from Oporto in 1899. Owner, Harvey & Co.
Snowbird:	80-ton schooner built at Liverpool in 1878. Lost in St. Mary's Bay in 1894. owner, Rorke.
Sparkling Glance:	217-ton tern built at Shelburn NS in 1916. Lost in the Atlantic in 1917. Owner, J. Harvey.
Spray:	Brigantine built in England in 1862. Lost at Torbay on a voyage from Alicante in 1868. Owner, Job Brothers.
Spencer Lake:	148-ton tern built in Fortune in 1920. Lost returning from Oporto in 1926. Owner, H.B. Lake.

Sperry: 95-ton schooner built at Lahave NS in 1900. Lost at St. Lawrence in 1907. Owner, Ryan.

Spinway: 95-ton schooner sunk off the Spanish coast by enemy U-boat in 1917.

Sprite: 130-ton schooner built in Indian Arm in 1867. Lost on a voyage to Cadiz in 1879. Owner, D. Sclater.

Spirit of the Times: Barque lost on a voyage from Liverpool in 1863. Owner, Ridley.

Stanley & Frank: 74-ton schooner built at Shelburne, NS in 1911. Lost in the Atlantic in 1920.

Stella: 221-ton barque built at Ayr, Scotland in 1893. Lost at Cuckolds Cove in 1904. Owner, J. Baird.

Stella 11: 356-ton tern built in Port Greville, NS in 1917. Lost off Algiers in 1920. Owner, J. Baird.

Stina: 191-ton tern built in Sweden in 1920. Lost off Portugal in 1934, Owner, W.W. Wareham.

Success: 199-ton tern built at Liverpool, NS in 1900. Lost off Portugal in 1919. Owner, J.S. Baird.

Sunner: 166-ton tern built in Notre Dame Bay, NL in 1919. Lost on a voyage from Turks Island in 1928. Captain

Thompson, his wife and two children and crew rescued and taken to Halifax.

Sunset Glow: 240-ton tern built at Shelburne, NS in 1916. Lost off Fogo in 1949. Owner, Harvey & Co.

Swallow: 85-ton schooner built at New Perlican, NL in 1877. Lost on voyage to New York in 1909. Owner, J. Munn.

Tattler: 100-ton schooner built in Essex, NS in 1901. Lost on voyage from Turks Island in 1918. Owner, Campbell & McKay.

Team Sixteen: 154-ton tern built at Coequid, NS in 1919. Lost in mid-Atlantic in 1920. Owner, Moulton.

Theresa Maud: 80-ton schooner built in Allendale, NS in 1912. Lost in mid-Atlantic in 1919. Owner, Thomas Ridley.

Thomas: 126-ton tern built in Norway in 1908. Sunk off Portugal by enemy U-boat in 1917. Owner, Harvey & Co.

Thomas A. Cromwell: 98-ton schooner built in Essex, NS in 1906. Lost on voyage to Spain in 1918. Owner, Tibbo

Thomas Ridley: 93-ton brig built in Carbonear, NL in 1852. Lost in ice tickles on a voyage to Gibraltar in 1885. Owner, J. Rorke.

Thomas W.: 99-ton tern built in Green's Harbour, NL in 1917. Lost off Barbados in 1919. Owner, G. Barr.

Tishey: 118-ton tern built in Placentia, NL in 1920. Lost near Greenspond in 1950. Owner, J. Baird.

Tobeatic: 99-ton tern built in Liverpool, NS in 1908. Lost on a return voyage from Gibraltar in 1914. Hickman & Randell.

Union Jack: 142-ton tern built in Trinity Bay, NL in 1918. Lost off Seldom in 1926. Owner, W.S. Monroe.

Valerie: 98-ton schooner built at Essex, NS in 1911. Lost on voyage from Cadiz in 1922. Owner, G. Harris.

Vanessa: 85-ton schooner built in Essex, NS in 1907. Lost in Atlantic in 1918 on a return voyage from Lisbon. Owner, W. Hollett.

Vidonia: 70-ton schooner built in Bath in 1867. Lost in Petty Harbour in 1905 on a voyage to Bahia. Owner, J. Patten.

Violet Buffett: 174-ton tern built in Marystown, NL in 1919. Lost off Burin on a return voyage from Portugal in 1920. owner, A. Buffett.

Violet Courtney: 128-ton tern built in Essex, NS in 1889. Lost in mid-Atlantic in 1917 on a voyage to Genoa. Owner, W. Courtney.

Violet May: 100-ton tern built in Mahone Bay, NS in 1913. Lost off St. Pierre in 1920 on a return voyage from Cadiz. Owner, J. Petite.

Virginia: 95-ton schooner built in Appledore, NS in 1904. Lost in the Atlantic in 1910. Owner, D. Ryan.

Virginia: 133-ton tern built in England in 1901. Lost in the Atlantic in 1912.

Virginia Lass: Brigantine lost in Nova Scotia in 1845. Owner, Harris.

Vogue: 196-ton tern built in Shelburne, NS in 1917. Lost in the Atlantic in 1921. Owner, A.E. Hickman.

Watanga: 100-ton schooner built in Lunenburg, NS in 1908. Burnt in Spain in 1918. Owner, W. Campbell.

Water Witch: 190-ton tern built in Liverpool, NS in 1906. Lost in 1918 off the Straits of Gibraltar. Owner, Crosbie.

W.H. Latimer:	185-ton brig built in Midway, Ns in 1875. Lost in the Atlantic in 1884. Owner, Bishop and Sons.
William:	74-ton brig built in Argyle in 1879. Struck by a meteorite and sank on a voyage from Oporto. Owner, Munn.
William:	116-ton brig lost of Cape St. Francis in 1842. Owner, Mudge.
William Donnelly:	Brig lost in 1878 at Renews.
Wilfred Marcus:	123-ton tern built in Shelburne, NS in 1914. Lost in 1918 on a return voyage from Portugal. Owner, G. Buffett.
William MacDonald:	252-ton tern built in Daysprings in 1920. Caught fire and was abandoned in mid-ocean.
William Morton:	145-ton tern built in Port Madoc, Wales in 1905. Lost on a return voyage from Cadiz in 1919. Owner, Harvey & Co.
William McL. Borden:	336-ton tern built in Pugwash, NS in 1919. Burnt at Ana-Mone, Portugal in 1919. Owner, Campbell.
Workman:	147-ton tern built in Charlottetown, NL in 1920. Lost through mid-Atlantic collision in 1922 on a voyage to Spain, Owner, A.E. Hickman.

Zebra: 142-ton tern built in Lahave, NS in 1867. Lost off the coast of Portugal in 1889.

APPENDIX II

OTHER SHIPS LOST IN THE FOREIGN FISH TRADE

(with only partial information about their tonnage, place of construction and owners)

Admiral Beatty: 100-ton schooner from Grand Bank lost near Grand Turks Island in 1931.

Armstrong: Tern lost in the Atlantic in 1923.

Benjamin Smith: Schooner lost on a voyage to Gibraltar in 1930.

Bessie Dodd: Vessel lost at St. Shott's on a return voyage from Cadiz in 1906.

Betoane: Motor vessel lost on a voyage from Barbados in 1941.

C.A. Hubley: Schooner lost on the east coast in 1937.

Canada: A vessel lost in the St. John's Narrows in 1810.

Canadian: Vessel owned by Bishop & Moore lost in 1900 on a voyage to Spain.

Charles W. Dalton: Brig lost at Golden Bay, St. Mary's Bay, on a voyage from Brazil in 1889.

Clive Moore: Tern lost of Cape St. Vincent in 1930.

Cora:	Vessel owned by Baine Johnston sunk in mid-Atlantic in 1880.
Corenso:	Tern sunk by enemy U-boat in 1916.
D. Chipman:	Barque lost at Witless Bay in 1879.
Danna:	A St. John's brigantine lost in the Atlantic in 1889.
Dave Morris:	Schooner lost at Turks Island in 1924.
Dellecnac:	Schooner lost in the Atlanti in 1919.
Douglas Adams:	A Twillingate schooner lost in mid-Atlantic on a return voyage from Portugal in 1921.
Earl Monsport:	Carbonear schooner foundered in 1948.
Elizabeth Llewellyn:	Tern lost in the Gibraltar area.
Emily Redmond:	Vessel lost in mid-Atlantic in 1885.
EMMA:	260-ton brig built in England. Lost at Flat Rock, 1885
Erna:	Steamship foundered in 1922.
Ethel:	Vessel lost in the Atlantic in 1918.
Ford River:	Schooner lost in the Atlantic in 1910.
Frank Adams:	Vessel lost in mid-Atlantic in 1923.
Feodre:	Vessel lost at Cape Spear in 1882 on a return voyage from Spain.
Harlet:	Schooner lost in the Mediterranean.

Hazel Myra:	Schooner owned by J. Munn lost in a fire off Bermuda in 1938.
Henry W. Adams:	Schooner sunk by enemy U-boat off the coast of Spain.
Ida:	Brigantine lost in the Channel Islands in 1855.
J.D. Hazen:	Schooner lost off Cape Lahave in 1934.
Jesse Costa:	83-ton schooner lost on a voyage from Boston in 1916.
J.R. Bradley:	Schooner lost in the Atlantic in 1919.
L.A.B.:	Schooner lost in the Atlantic in 1916.
Laurel:	Schooner lost at Lamaline in 1863 on a voyage from New York.
Lavengro:	269-ton tern built in Shelburne, NS in 1909. Lost off Fogo Island on a voyage to Spain.
Maggie Bell:	Schooner lost off the Azores in 1917. Owner, G. Barr.
Margaret Schartz:	89-ton schooner lost in St. Mary's Bay in 1915
Maria:	St. John's brigantine lost in the Atlantic in 1889.
Mayola:	Tern, sunk by enemy U-boat off the coast of Portugal in 1917.

Niaza:	Schooner lost in mid-Atlantic. Owner, Wight.
Norma:	St. John's barquentine lost in the Atlantic in 1889.
Northumberland:	Vessel lost in mid Atlantic in 1873.
Olive Branch:	Brig lost at Petty Harbour in 1822 on a voyage from Oporto.
Rosallin:	Schooner lost in the Atlantic in 1923.
Speedwell 11:	Schooner lost at Algiers in 1917.
Susan:	Barquentine lost near Cape Broyle on a voyage to the West Indies in 1887.
Thomas Edward:	Brig burnt in a fire off Cape St. Francis on a voyage to Hamburg.
Thomas Harvey:	A St. John's vessel lost on a return voyage from Cadiz in 1917.
Titania:	Brig lost at Cape Spear in 1880 on a voyage to Miramichi.
W.T. White:	99-ton schooner lost on a voyage to Santa Pola in 1920.
William Donnelly:	Brig lost off Renews in 1885.

BIBLIOGRAPHY

BOOKS:

Andrieux, J.P., Marine Disasters and Shipwrecks of Newfoundland and Labrador, Volumes 1& 2, St. John's, 1986 & 1992.

Bartlett, Bob, Captain, The Log of Bob Bartlett, New York, 1928.

Devine & Lawton, Old King's Cove, St. John's, 1944.

Divine & O'Mara, Noteable Events, St. John's, 1900.

Fay, C.R., Life and Labour in Newfoundland, Toronto, 1956.

Horwood, Andrew, Newfoundland Ships and Men, St. John's, 1971.

Innis, Harold, The Cod Fishery, Toronto, 1954.

Kean, Abram, Captain, Old and Young Ahead, London, 1935.

Keir, David, The Bowring Story, London 1962.

Mosdell, H.M., When Was That? St. John's 1923.

Parsons, Robert, Lost at Sea Volume 1, St, John's, 1991, Volume 2,1992, Toll of the Sea, St. John's, 1995, Survive The Savage Sea, St. John's, 1998.

Ryan, Shannon, Fish Out of Water, St. John's, 1986.

Zinc Jack, Shipwrecks of Nova Scotia, Volume 1, Windsor, Nova Scotia, 1975, Volume 2, 1977.

NEWSPAPERS:

Chronicle: May 30, 1909.

Daily News: January 18, 1904, May 18, 1904, February 19, 1917, December 8, 1921, January 4, 1922, January 16, 1922, October 17, 1923, March 24, 1926, December 6, 1927, January 20, 1940.

Evening Telegram: May 12, 1885, March 28, 1887, May 6, 1892, May 18, 1904, January 16, 1905, February 11, 1905, January 18, 1909, January 22, 1989, May 20, 1909, June 7, 1909, February 19, 1919, October 18, 1919, February 26, 1920, September 5, 1921, March 6, 1923, February 15, 1924, September 29, 1925, February 11, 1930, January 20, 1935, February 2, 1935.

Evening Herald: August 6, 1897, January 8, 1910, February 6, 1914, March 17, 1917,May 28, 1919.

Newfoundlander: March 22, 1872.

Public Ledger: January 12, 1869.

Times: March 2, 1881, November 3, 1883.

Trade Review: March 10, 1923, March 14, 1924, December 6, 1930, January 4, 1931.

LIST OF ILLUSTRATED SHIPS

INDEX

ABOUT THE AUTHORS

CAPTAIN JOE PRIM was born in St. John's, Newfoundland. He went to sea in 1943 at age 16 and served for nine years in the foreign trade. He served for twenty-four years as master of various CN vessels, including the *William Carson* and the *Ambrose Shea*. In 1985 he was appointed Assistant Marine Superintendent and served in that capacity until his retirement in 1990. He has published several charts of shipwrecks and ships sunk by enemy action along the Newfoundland and Labrador coast, and he has written articles on navigational changes to shipping along the coast. He is co-author of two books, *Those in Peril* and *The Angry Sea*. Captain Joe Prim is married to the former Geraldine O'Brien of Cape Broyle. They have seven children and presently reside in St. John's.

MICHAEL J. MCCARTHY was born in St. Jacques, Fortune Bay, moving to Terrenceville at the age of five, where he attended school until grade XI. He attended Memorial University of Newfoundland and the University of Ottawa, graduating with an M.A. degree in Literature. He taught in a number of communities until his retirement in 1986. Mike is the author of three novels: *The Journey Home*, *The Treasure of Kelly's Island* and *Escape*, together with a history of *The Irish in Newfoundland*. He has co-authored *Shipwrecks of Newfoundland and Labrador*, *The Angry Seas*, *A Christmas Box*, *Fables, Fairies and Folklore*, *Buried Treasures of Newfoundland and Labrador*, *Olde St. John's*, *A Sea of Mother's Tears*, and a history of communications called *Voice of Generations*. Mr. McCarthy has also written for several magazines, as well as radio and television. He is married to the former Ann Hamlyn and has two children: Michael and Karen. He resides in Mount Pearl.